OPPOSING
VIEWPOINTS®
SERIES

The US Military

Other Books of Related Interest:

Opposing Viewpoints Series

Domestic Terrorism

US Foreign Policy

Veterans

World Peace

At Issue Series

Biological and Chemical Weapons

Domestic Surveillance

Drones

Current Controversies Series

Military Families

Espionage and Intelligence

Gays in the Military

"Congress shall make no law ... abridging the freedom of speech, or of the press."

First Amendment to the US Constitution

The basic foundation of our democracy is the First Amendment guarantee of freedom of expression. The Opposing Viewpoints series is dedicated to the concept of this basic freedom and the idea that it is more important to practice it than to enshrine it.

OPPOSING
VIEWPOINTS®
SERIES

The US Military

Noah Berlatsky, Book Editor

GREENHAVEN PRESS
A part of Gale, Cengage Learning

GALE
CENGAGE Learning·

Farmington Hills, Mich • San Francisco • New York • Waterville, Maine
Meriden, Conn • Mason, Ohio • Chicago

Judy Galens, *Manager, Frontlist Acquisitions*

For more information, contact:
Greenhaven Press
27500 Drake Rd.
Farmington Hills, MI 48331-3535
Or you can visit our Internet site at gale.cengage.com

LIBRARY OF CONGRESS CATALOGING-IN-PUBLICATION DATA

The US military / Noah Berlatsky, book editor.
    pages cm. -- -- (Opposing viewpoints)
    Includes bibliographical references and index.
    ISBN 978-0-7377-7566-2 (hardcover) -- ISBN 978-0-7377-7567-9 (pbk.)
    1. United States--Military policy. 2. United States--Armed Forces. I. Berlatsky, Noah, editor. II. Title: The U.S. military. III. Title: The United States military.
    UA23.U2226 2016
    355'.033573--dc23
                        2015021389

Printed in the United States of America
    1 2 3 4 5   19 18 17 16 15

Contents

Chapter 3: What Are US Military Personnel Issues?

Why Consider Opposing Viewpoints?

> *"The only way in which a human being can make some approach to knowing the whole of a subject is by hearing what can be said about it by persons of every variety of opinion and studying all modes in which it can be looked at by every character of mind. No wise man ever acquired his wisdom in any mode but this."*
>
> *John Stuart Mill*

In our media-intensive culture it is not difficult to find differing opinions. Thousands of newspapers and magazines and dozens of radio and television talk shows resound with differing points of view. The difficulty lies in deciding which opinion to agree with and which "experts" seem the most credible. The more inundated we become with differing opinions and claims, the more essential it is to hone critical reading and thinking skills to evaluate these ideas. Opposing Viewpoints books address this problem directly by presenting stimulating debates that can be used to enhance and teach these skills. The varied opinions contained in each book examine many different aspects of a single issue. While examining these conveniently edited opposing views, readers can develop critical thinking skills such as the ability to compare and contrast authors' credibility, facts, argumentation styles, use of persuasive techniques, and other stylistic tools. In short, the Opposing Viewpoints Series is an ideal way to attain the higher-level thinking and reading skills so essential in a culture of diverse and contradictory opinions.

In addition to providing a tool for critical thinking, Opposing Viewpoints books challenge readers to question their own strongly held opinions and assumptions. Most people form their opinions on the basis of upbringing, peer pressure, and personal, cultural, or professional bias. By reading carefully balanced opposing views, readers must directly confront new ideas as well as the opinions of those with whom they disagree. This is not to argue simplistically that everyone who reads opposing views will—or should—change his or her opinion. Instead, the series enhances readers' understanding of their own views by encouraging confrontation with opposing ideas. Careful examination of others' views can lead to the readers' understanding of the logical inconsistencies in their own opinions, perspective on why they hold an opinion, and the consideration of the possibility that their opinion requires further evaluation.

Evaluating Other Opinions

To ensure that this type of examination occurs, Opposing Viewpoints books present all types of opinions. Prominent spokespeople on different sides of each issue as well as well-known professionals from many disciplines challenge the reader. An additional goal of the series is to provide a forum for other, less known, or even unpopular viewpoints. The opinion of an ordinary person who has had to make the decision to cut off life support from a terminally ill relative, for example, may be just as valuable and provide just as much insight as a medical ethicist's professional opinion. The editors have two additional purposes in including these less known views. One, the editors encourage readers to respect others' opinions—even when not enhanced by professional credibility. It is only by reading or listening to and objectively evaluating others' ideas that one can determine whether they are worthy of consideration. Two, the inclusion of such viewpoints encourages the important critical thinking skill of objectively evaluating an author's credentials and bias. This evaluation will illuminate an author's reasons for taking a particular stance on an issue and will aid in readers' evaluation of the author's ideas.

It is our hope that these books will give readers a deeper understanding of the issues debated and an appreciation of the complexity of even seemingly simple issues when good and honest people disagree. This awareness is particularly important in a democratic society such as ours in which people enter into public debate to determine the common good. Those with whom one disagrees should not be regarded as enemies but rather as people whose views deserve careful examination and may shed light on one's own.

Thomas Jefferson once said that "difference of opinion leads to inquiry, and inquiry to truth." Jefferson, a broadly educated man, argued that "if a nation expects to be ignorant and free . . . it expects what never was and never will be." As individuals and as a nation, it is imperative that we consider the opinions of others and examine them with skill and discernment. The Opposing Viewpoints series is intended to help readers achieve this goal.

David L. Bender and Bruno Leone,
Founders

Introduction

"Military satellite communications have become essential to help the warfighter see through the 'fog of war,' providing the United States military with assured global connectivity, even in remote areas with no communications infrastructure."

—Mak King and
Michael J. Riccio, "Military Satellite
Communications: Then and Now,"
Aerospace, December 12, 2013

In March 2015, a two-decade-old US military satellite experienced a sudden spike in temperature, and then it exploded. The satellite was no longer being used to monitor weather, and officials said that the tactical impact of the explosion was minimal. The satellite seems to have exploded because of old age rather than because of any sort of attack. Still, the sudden explosion highlights the fact that military satellites are an important component of US defense—and that those satellites can be vulnerable. Satellites allow the US military to maintain communications around the globe; they provide intelligence by pinpointing enemies; and they enable weapons guidance. It is not likely that they will all spontaneously explode, luckily—but if they did, the security of the United States would be in peril.

For awhile, the United States was more or less alone in its control of space and did not have to worry about its satellites being taken out by opposing forces. Still today, the United States has more than five hundred satellites in space, many more than any other nation.

While US superiority remains, its invulnerability does not. China, most notably, "has been actively testing anti-satellite weapons that could, in effect, knock out America's eyes and ears," said CBS's David Martin. China and Russia, in fact, have been working on anti-satellite technologies, while other countries, including Iran and North Korea, can launch objects into space. General John Hyten, the head of Air Force Space Command at Peterson Air Force Base in Colorado, said in the CBS interview with Martin in April 2015 that "it's a competition that I wish wasn't occurring, but it is. And if we're threatened in space, we have the right of self-defense, and we'll make sure we can execute that right."

Hyten added that China is quickly developing the capability to attack US satellites throughout the sky. Some satellites may have the ability to maneuver away from an anti-satellite weapon; some, though, do not. "It depends on the satellite," Hyten said. "When it was built . . . how old it is . . . when we know the threat is coming."

This new competition has major consequences for how the military creates and uses satellites. Most notably, current satellites are big, bulky, and very expensive—some can cost as much as an aircraft carrier. That means that if a single satellite were rendered inoperable, it would be very, very hard to replace it quickly—or even at all. The military is therefore trying to figure out how to build smaller, lighter satellites that can "quickly respond to a military commander's needs, bypassing the normal decades-long multibillion dollar hassle," according to Steven Tomaszewski at VICE News.

To make these smaller satellites effective requires getting them into orbit as well, and the military is therefore trying to develop launch strategies. Currently, Tomaszewski said, the best bet is called the Minotaur, an altered ballistic missile that has been converted into a launch vehicle that can carry a satellite into orbit.

When a satellite explodes, or when military commanders discuss the threat of another country taking out an American satellite, it can be easy to feel like America's defenses are vulnerable. Andrew Browne in the *Wall Street Journal,* however, argued in May 2015 that the threat can easily be overstated. Browne said that even though China is developing anti-satellite technology, "it itself is becoming increasingly reliant on space for battlefield intelligence, and therefore similarly vulnerable" to space-based attacks. Chinese missiles, for example, need satellite guidance to reach their target. Furthermore, "as Chinese missile technology advances, so does America's ability to defend," according to Browne.

It is important to realize that the US military spends $25 billion a year on space; that is more than the National Aeronautics and Space Administration (NASA) and any other space program, civilian or military, in the world. That $25 billion is thought to be around ten times as much as China spends on its space program. In space, as in every other area, the United States invests vastly more than any other country on earth. The question of whether America is spending enough to defend itself in space, then, seems like it should be balanced with the question of whether America is spending too much on defense.

Opposing Viewpoints: The US Military examines other issues important to the US armed forces in chapters titled "Should the US Military Budget Be Reduced?," "In What Conflicts Should the United States Intervene?," "What Are US Military Personnel Issues?," and "How Is the United States Caring for Its Veterans?"

Each chapter provides multiple viewpoints on issues vital to the US military and the country it serves.

CHAPTER 1

Should the US Military Budget Be Reduced?

Chapter Preface

For many years, the Pentagon has tried to close excess military bases to save money, manpower, and resources. In April 2015, for example, a Department of Defense (DOD) facilities official testified in Congress on the need for base closings. The official quoted the deputy secretary of defense, Robert O. Work, who is responsible for the efficient management of the Department of Defense, who said, "in this time of constrained resources, I just don't understand why we are hamstringing ourselves [keeping unnecessary bases open]. Maintaining that extra capacity is a big problem for us because it's wasteful spending, period. It is the worst type of bloat."

Congress claims that it wants to reduce waste in the Defense Department. However, when the DOD provides a concrete example of waste it wants to cut, Congress inevitably balks. As just one example, New Jersey lawmakers were afraid that proposed base closings would include the Joint Base McGuire-Dix-Lakehurst. The lawmakers, including congressmen Tom MacArthur and Donald Norcross, not only scrapped the provisions for base closings but also prevented the Pentagon from spending money to move the KC-10 refueling tankers from the bases. MacArthur said that "the KC-10 is critically important not only to our military's air mobility and readiness, but to the survival of Joint Base McGuire-Dix-Lakehurst and the 40,000 New Jerseyans employed there."

Though MacArthur talks about national security, it seems likely that a big part of the incentive to keep the bases open for politicians is those forty thousand jobs. Members of Congress never want to see bases close because they never want to lose jobs in their districts. As a result, the Defense Department has had to look elsewhere to reduce bloat. In January 2015, for example, the department moved to close bases in Europe—since Europe, of course, has no congressional representation. Dozens of bases in Britain, Germany, Belgium, the Netherlands, Italy, and Portugal were slated for closure, with projected savings of half a billion dollars.

In some cases, the Defense Department may actually be able to close bases without congressional approval. There are legal provisions for DOD officials to shut down bases merely by notifying Congress. Military.com reported that House Armed Services Committee staffer Vickie Plunkett stated at an Association of the United States Army conference in 2014 that if the DOD were willing to take the political risk, it could close facilities without getting permission from Congress. She said, "The Secretary of the Army has unilateral authority . . . to close arsenals. . . . Now the issue is will the services . . . take advantage of those statutes?" So far DOD has not, but perhaps eventually, if Congress refuses to act, it may resort to such tactics.

The authors of the viewpoints in the following chapter examine other issues surrounding military budgeting, such as whether the United States needs to spend more or less money on defense, the effects of sequestration on the military, and using defense spending to create jobs.

"Voters clearly believe the focus should be more on defending the United States rather than the whole world."

The US Military Budget Should Be Reduced

Scott Rasmussen

Scott Rasmussen is the founder and president of Rasmussen Reports and the author of The People's Money: How Voters Will Balance the Budget and Eliminate the Federal Debt. *In the following viewpoint, he argues that American spending on defense is excessive and far beyond what the American people feel is necessary. He says that the United States should stop trying to police the world and should instead move to a "Protect America First" strategy, maintaining a military large enough to protect the homeland. Rasmussen argues that this will contribute to economic stability and will ultimately make America more secure.*

As you read, consider the following questions:

1. According to Rasmussen, in 2011 what percentage of the American public favored finding spending cuts in all government programs?

2. According to the viewpoint, what did Admiral Mike Mullen say was "the most significant threat" to America's national security?

3. Rasmussen wants to return military spending to the levels of what year?

In July [2012] presumptive Republican presidential nominee Mitt Romney wrote an open letter to Barack Obama slamming the president for considering Pentagon cuts. "Your insistence on slashing our military to pay the tab for your irresponsible spending could see over 200,000 troops forced from service," Romney warned. "It will shut the doors on factories and shipyards that support our warfighters, take a heavy toll on the guard and reserves, and potentially shutter Virginia military bases. It will shrink our Navy below a level that is already not adequate for protecting our national security." Romney, by contrast, promises to spend at least 4 percent of gross domestic product on defense every year during his tenure.

Republicans who demand cuts in every program except the military open themselves up to justifiable Democratic charges of hypocrisy. Exempting major budget categories from spending discipline is a key reason government almost never gets cut. The American people are ready to take a more mature approach. A 2011 poll conducted by my firm, Rasmussen Reports, found that 67 percent favor finding spending cuts in all government programs. Every budget item, Americans emphatically believe, needs to be on the table.

A Difficult Discussion

National security is a difficult topic to discuss in mere budgetary terms, since Americans are understandably uncomfortable with putting a price tag on safety. As [former president] Ronald Reagan once put it, "Defense is not a budget issue. You spend what you need."

Reagan's attitude was correct in one basic sense: If we can't defend the nation, nothing else matters. But it is also important to remember that he was speaking in a particular place and time. Recognizing that the Soviet economy could not keep up with the more vibrant U.S. economy, he was seeking to put financial pressure on the Communist empire and hasten its collapse. That Reagan succeeded is one of the reasons we can consider different approaches in the 21st century.

Today we face no rival superpower with massive military capabilities and aggressive ambitions. Threats of terrorism and cyberwarfare are real but stem mostly from small cells, rather than large blocs of countries. Still, defense spending questions are hard to discuss because most Americans hold a jumble of conflicting emotions and perceptions that cloud the debate and shift the focus to almost everything except money.

As a starting point, Americans are proud of their country and hold its armed forces in high regard. Seventy-nine percent would rather live here than anywhere else, and at a time of deep cynicism about large institutions, 81 percent have a favorable opinion of the U.S. military.

Yet this respect and admiration for the troops coexists with doubts about the jobs they've been asked to do. Most voters now believe it was a mistake for the U.S. to have gotten involved in Iraq [in 2003], and most now want to see troops brought home quickly from Afghanistan. Support for the military action in Libya [in 2011] peaked at 20 percent.

Americans are also in a mood to dramatically reduce our security guarantees for other nations. Less than half (49 percent) believe the U.S. should remain in its bedrock military alliance, NATO [North Atlantic Treaty Organization]. Out of 54 countries with which Washington has signed mutual-defense treaty obligations, plus two others (Israel and Mexico) that receive our implicit backing, a majority of Americans support defending just 12. Countries that don't reach the 50 percent threshold include our oldest ally, France, along with Japan, Poland, and Denmark. The only four countries that 60 percent of Americans are willing to defend are Canada, the United Kingdom, Australia, and Israel.

These findings highlight the central 21st-century gap between the citizenry and its political class. Three out of four Americans believe U.S. troops should never be deployed for military action overseas unless vital national security interests are at stake. Yet the last several presidents have adopted far less restrictive criteria for sending troops abroad. The military is often dispatched for humanitarian purposes or in the belief that the U.S. should police the world, but only 11 percent of voters believe Uncle Sam should play global cop.

Despite how some may interpret these numbers, voters are not isolationists. They still want Washington to play a leading role in world affairs; they see their country as a force for good and reject those who tend to blame America first for the planet's woes. But citizens equally reject the default Washington position that we should respond to international crises by sending Americans first. Instead, voters are seeking a strategy that might best be described as Protect America First. If the military is successful in its core duty of protecting the nation, they believe, our other national assets will win over hearts and minds around the globe.

This mix of public attitudes suggests it is possible to develop a popular 21st-century defense strategy that will support the troops and protect the nation while reducing annual military spending by hundreds of billions of dollars.

What America Spends Now

In 2010 the federal government spent more than $875 billion on national defense and veterans affairs, around one-fourth of the federal budget. That figure included about $160 billion for overseas contingency operations, which consisted mostly of the wars in Iraq and Afghanistan, plus $155 billion for the direct costs of military personnel and $31 billion to care for "wounded, ill, and injured" service members and their families. Veterans' benefits and services total about $125 billion, including $45 billion for health care. Maintaining a military with 1.4 million active-duty personnel, it turns out, is expensive.

In addition to military personnel and veterans, the national security budget includes nearly 800,000 civilian personnel. That number does not include the people working for the Department of Homeland Security and other defense-related agencies.

For most people, these numbers are simply too big to fathom. One way of contextualizing the cost is by looking at how fast the national security budget has grown during the last decade. In 2001, the year of the horrific 9/11 terrorist attacks [referring to the September 11 terrorist attacks on the United States], the federal government spent about $350 billion on defense and veterans affairs. If that spending had kept pace with the growth in population and inflation, it would total about $481 billion today. Current spending is 82 percent higher than that. It is no surprise that defense budgets increased after 9/11, but it is legitimate to ask if an 82 percent hike was the right amount.

Military spending today, adjusted for population and inflation, is higher than it was when Ronald Reagan left office—a time when the Soviet empire was still pointing nuclear weapons at U.S. cities. It is higher than it was in 1968, when the U.S. was fighting both the Cold War and a deadly hot war in Vietnam. Although Americans will support spending whatever it takes to defend the country, polling suggests they don't realize how much we're spending right now.

Only 58 percent of voters are aware that the United States spends more on defense than any other country in the world. And just 33 percent recognize that Washington spends roughly as much on defense as the rest of the world combined. Mili-

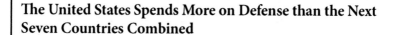

The United States Spends More on Defense than the Next Seven Countries Combined

Defense Spending (billions of dollars)

$601 Billion — China, Russia, Saudi Arabia, France, United Kingdom, India, Germany

$610 Billion — United States

Source: Stockholm International Peace Research Institute, *SIPRI Military Expenditure Database*, April 2015. Data are for 2014. Compiled by PGPF.
Note: Figures are in US dollars, converted from local currencies using market exchange rates.

TAKEN FROM: Peter G. Peterson Foundation, "The U.S. Spends More on Defense than the Next Seven Countries Combined," April 13, 2015.

tary spending has grown disproportionately compared to Americans' own priorities, dwarfing other countries in ways that could soon make taxpayers blink.

Consider: The United States spends more than $2,500 per person on national defense; Russia and our NATO allies each spend about one-fifth that amount, at a time when only 46 percent of Americans have a favorable view of NATO. In the aggregate, while the U.S. is spending close to $900 billion a year on the military and veterans affairs, China is coughing up less than $200 billion. North Korea, Iran, and Syria combined spend less than $30 billion. The Pentagon spends more just on research and development than Germany, the United Kingdom, France, Russia, and Japan each spend on their entire defense budgets, according to Cato Institute vice president Christopher A. Preble's 2009 book *The Power Problem*. If we are at risk militarily, it is certainly not for a lack of spending.

Adm. Mike Mullen, then chairman of the Joint Chiefs of Staff, said in 2010 that "the most significant threat to our national security is our debt." The American people agree: 82 percent believe the economy is now a bigger concern than military challenges. Sooner rather than later, defense spending will have to come back in line with voter desires.

What to Cut

As with just about every aspect of the federal budget crisis, the main question is whether the political class will continue pursuing its own agenda or be forced to accept the commonsense wisdom of the American people. Following the logic of the public's strategic preferences would lead to tremendous savings on defense. Americans, like their political representatives, are not isolationists; 88 percent say the country's relationship with Europe is important, for example, and 53 percent say it's "very" important. Voters have no expressed desire to retreat from our historical idealism and sympathy for people who believe in liberty and freedom. It's just that the citizenry rejects the political class's post–Cold War approach to pursuing these ideals.

A Protect America First policy would mean returning to the more restrained military philosophies of Dwight Eisenhower and Ronald Reagan. Those presidents did not hesitate to use force, but they had a more limited definition of when it was appropriate: only when vital U.S. interests were at stake.

Reagan articulated additional restrictions. Forces should not be sent without "the clear intent and support needed to win," or without "clearly defined and realistic objectives." And there "must be reasonable assurance that the cause we are fighting for and the actions we take will have the support of the American people and Congress." Even when those criteria were met, Reagan emphasized that "our troops should be committed to combat abroad only as a last resort." Although the Gipper himself occasionally fell short of those ideals (circumventing Congress in Central America, for example), Americans today firmly back the guidelines he spelled out.

Aligning U.S. military strategy with public opinion would save trillions of dollars during the coming decade and dramatically reduce the debt burden we are imposing on future generations. This important realignment would put us in a better position to deal with the serious economic challenges facing the nation and reaffirm the bedrock American notion that governments derive their only just authority from the consent of the governed.

Protect America First

Still, it won't be easy, given the emotions and vested interests involved. One way to tackle the problem is by breaking defense spending into its constituent chunks.

Supplemental Budget Requests. The supplemental budget for operations in Afghanistan and Iraq cost the United States $163 billion in 2010 and $181 billion in 2011. The Obama administration plans to reduce this number to about $118 billion in 2012.

Most Americans have decided that it's time to bring these troops home within a year, much faster than either major political party currently contemplates. While such a withdrawal would need to take battlefield concerns into account, bringing policy more in line with public desires could save hundreds of billions of dollars.

Baseline Military Budget. General military spending, or the baseline budget, totaled about $530 billion for 2011.

The only way to substantially reduce that number is through strategic cuts in troop levels and deployments, which could take years and may not begin to show up in reduced budgets for five or 10 years.

Still, the biggest savings available here can be found in the yawning gap between the 56 nations we are obliged to protect and the 12 countries a majority of Americans support defending. If the global mission is reduced, the cost will be too. Simply put, fewer troops are needed to defend the United States than are needed to police the world. Just bringing home U.S. troops currently deployed in Western Europe and Japan would result in direct savings of about $25 billion per year.

Defense Secretary Robert Gates acknowledged in 2010 at the Navy League's Sea-Air-Space exposition "the massive overmatch the U.S. already enjoys," asking: "Do we really need 11 carrier strike groups for another 30 years when no other country has more than one? Any future plans must address these realities." A Protect America First strategy would concentrate fleets closer to home and reduce the number of aircraft carriers, airplanes, submarines, support staff, and sailors.

All of these changes would reduce procurement budgets because the military wouldn't need as many new weapons, ships, and aircraft each year. Considering that there are more than 80 weapons systems that cost more than $1 billion a year, reducing procurement would lead to real savings overnight. Training and recruiting costs would also go down, as would administrative costs and the number of civilian support personnel.

Veterans Affairs. If we cut back on the number of soldiers today, we cut back on the number of veterans we need to serve in the future. If we suffer fewer casualties now, we will have fewer disability payments, lower medical costs, and fewer survivors' benefits in the future.

It sounds pretty basic, and it is. But the impact is huge. By reducing the number of soldiers today, we will reduce the total spending burden we are passing on to future generations by trillions of dollars. Consider these facts, from Cato's Christopher Preble: "Of the 700,000 men and women who served in the Gulf War, 45 percent filed for disability benefits, and 88 percent of these requests were approved. On average, disabled Gulf War veterans receive $6,506 every year; this amounts to $4.3 billion paid out annually by the U.S. government." That's the cost paid every year for veterans of just one military engagement.

The savings won't show up right away in reduced budgets, since today's budget reflects the price we pay for yesterday's veterans. But as with other unfunded liabilities, that accounting issue says more about the faulty way we measure federal budgets and deficits than it does about the magnitude of the savings.

A New Balance

By reducing the number of strategic commitments in places such as Europe and Japan, we can return military spending to 2001 levels, adjusted for population and inflation. Some might balk at setting targets for defense spending and then expecting the military to fit within those parameters, but that's exactly what Dwight Eisenhower did in the 1950s. Ike recognized the need to balance military power with domestic resources. It would be irrational to demand that the military continue policing the world with a reduced budget, but it is quite rational to expect the military to accomplish the narrower mission of Protect America First with a budget appropriate for that role.

These reductions would still allow around $420 billion in annual military spending, nearly three times as much as what China or anybody else in the world currently shells out. And that spending level would be much more in line with voter preferences. If anything, it might be a bit on the high side: Just 25 percent of voters believe the United States should always spend at least three times as much as any other nation; 40 percent think such a target is excessive.

Once the initial cutbacks and savings have been fully implemented over five to 10 years, it would be essential to set in place some long-term budgetary discipline within a more rational federal spending outlook. As long as the strategic environment remains the same, annual military spending increases should be pegged to population growth and inflation. If a new military rival emerged, obviously, it would be time for a new strategic assessment.

But as of 2012, it's difficult to envision a serious military rival that could threaten the territory of the United States.

There is no magic to choosing the 2001 defense budget as a starting point, but it does have the advantage of clarifying the strategic choices. If we spend as much today as we did in 2001 but reduce our legacy commitments from the World War II era, we could cut overall spending levels while devoting additional resources to fighting the challenges of the post–9/11 world.

The specifics of how to recalculate defense spending should be the focus of intense debate and experimentation. Voters clearly believe the focus should be more on defending the United States rather than the whole world. Substantial resources would still be deployed to address the terrorist threat and probably also to help secure the southern border of the United States.

Many on both sides of the partisan and ideological divides will be unhappy with this approach to military spending. That's especially true of a political elite that supports the Send Americans First status quo. For them, there is a simple solution: If you don't like the Protect America First strategy, go to your boss, the American people. If there are arguments to be made for a wider U.S. engagement and for interventions in places such as Libya, make them. If there are reasons to leave U.S. troops in Europe forever, state them. If we need to spend more, build support for the taxes needed to finance that spending.

But don't sacrifice America's greatest asset—our commitment to self-governance—to pursue a far more aggressive and costly military strategy than the American people are willing to support. Americans have rejected Washington's bipartisan foreign policy. It's time for politicians to take the hint.

> "Congress should reform entitlement spending, reduce non-defense discretionary spending, and prioritize its core constitutional function to provide for the common defense."

The US Military Budget Should Be Increased

Diem Nguyen Salmon

Diem Nguyen Salmon is senior policy analyst for defense budgeting at the Heritage Foundation. In the following viewpoint, she argues that defense spending has fallen dangerously in recent years. Cuts to spending have degraded US forces, she says, and many new threats make the world more dangerous for the United States. She suggests an increase in defense spending over several years and recommends a decrease in non-defense spending to balance the budget.

As you read, consider the following questions:

1. What two factors does Salmon cite in support of increasing defense spending?

2. What new threats does the United States face since 2008, according to Salmon?

3. What defense programs does Salmon say were cut in fiscal years 2014 and 2015, respectively?

U.S. foreign and defense policy has reached a critical juncture. In an astonishingly brief period of time, the world—and America's place in it—has changed dramatically. During this period, presidential elections, the financial crisis, and government shutdown politics largely supplanted overseas engagements and foreign affairs in the minds of the White House and Congress. The swearing in of a new Congress and a new majority party in the Senate provides an important opportunity to reassess the objectives of U.S. foreign policy and to align other policy priorities accordingly. The U.S. defense budget is the first among the items to reconsider in the context of a changing international landscape. While foreign policy matters cannot simply be solved with more money for defense, little can be expected to change without it.

Consecutive years of across-the-board budget cuts have significantly weakened the U.S. military. The military will likely need several years of reinvestment to return to a sound footing, and a higher defense budget for fiscal year (FY) 2016 would be an encouraging start.

To that end, for FY 2016, Congress should increase the discretionary caps on defense instituted by the Budget Control Act of 2011 (BCA). *Specifically, Congress should allocate $584 billion to defense spending for FY 2016.* At the same time, Congress should put America on a path to fiscal responsibility and safeguard national security by reducing deficits and the national debt. Congress's repeated failures to address out-of-control entitlement spending, the real driver of unsustainable federal spending, means that the BCA's spending cuts will be short-lived, hampering necessary growth in defense spending. Instead of the status quo, Congress should reform entitlement spending, reduce non-defense discretionary spending, and prioritize its core constitutional function to provide for the common defense.

The Case for Increasing Defense Spending

Two factors justify increasing defense spending:

First, the security situation in many parts of the world has shifted in directions unfavorable to U.S. interests. In the past few years, the constellation of threats to the U.S. has changed, and the U.S. needs to reexamine current defense spending levels, which were set in 2011.

Second, the state of the U.S. military continues to degrade due to recent spending decisions. The several years of uncertainty in the defense budget, the un-prioritized cuts, and the magnitude and pace of the reductions have led to a weaker and smaller force today. . . .

In 2008, then senator Barack Obama (D-IL) campaigned on ending the war in Iraq among other issues, and a slight majority of Americans agreed. For better or for worse, the prevailing sentiment was that it was time to end unnecessary military engagements abroad and refocus on domestic issues—on "nation-building here at home."

In 2009, President Obama began his first term in the White House, and the Democratic Party controlled both the Senate and the House of Representatives. That same year, in line with his campaign promise, President Obama announced plans to withdraw all U.S. troops from Iraq. A decision to reduce the number of troops in Afghanistan would follow in 2011.

President Obama also announced his Russian "reset" policy, based on the notion that the Cold War was over and the U.S. needed to start warming relations with Russia. As part of the reset policy, the U.S. reduced the number of troops based in Europe. Considerations for reduction in defense spending began at the same time.

Reality soon intruded on President Obama's desire to focus solely on domestic concerns, beginning with Tunisia in December 2010. The Arab Spring protest movement, which affected every country in the Middle East and North Africa to varying degrees, ousted several regional leaders from power and upended the existing geopolitical dynamics in the Middle East. Instability and unrest persist in many of these countries—including Libya, Egypt, and Yemen—with little promise of resolution or stability anywhere on the horizon.

Fragile as those countries are, the legacy of the Arab Spring is nowhere more painfully evident than in border areas of Iraq and Syria. The March 2011 uprising against [Syrian leader] Bashar al-Assad, Assad's violent response, and the increasing sectarian strife in Iraq after the withdrawal of American troops would have been unwelcome developments on their own merits, but the turmoil in Iraq and the burgeoning civil war in Syria also paved the way for the emergence of the Islamist terrorist organization known as the Islamic State [of Iraq and Syria] (ISIS).

ISIS has plunged the region back into widespread armed conflict and turmoil, affecting millions of lives. Large areas of Syria and Iraq are now under ISIS control, while Turkey, Lebanon, and Jordan are facing a refugee crisis. As the president stated, "if left unchecked, these terrorists could pose a growing threat beyond that region, including to the United States."

In Russia, Vladimir Putin's invasion and annexation of the Crimean peninsula in April 2014 proved that the talk of a "reset" of relations with Russia was an entirely one-sided narrative. The continuing conflict in eastern Ukraine has cost thousands of Ukrainian lives, and no end is in sight. The stability and relative regional security that European countries had enjoyed since the implosion of the Soviet Union is now very much in doubt.

Other pressing issues include the Ebola epidemic in West Africa; the growing strength of terrorist groups affiliated with al Qaeda and ISIS, in failed states and ungoverned spaces around the globe, particularly in Africa; China's increasing displays of aggressiveness; cyber-warfare; and the persistent threat of a nuclear Iran.

Not all of these situations require military intervention, but they do require an acknowledgement that the existing world order bears little resemblance to the one at the beginning of the Obama administration. In many ways, as noted by the Chairman of the Joint Chiefs of Staff, General Martin E. Dempsey, the world has become more dangerous, and the United States needs to reevaluate its military posture based on a clear-eyed assessment of current threats.

Response and Responsibilities

While there is a significant debate about how to respond to these developments, most in Washington recognize these situations for what they are—threats to U.S. interests—and have once again turned to the military for solutions, placing new demands on an already stressed force. To counter Russia, the U.S. is returning some of the previously withdrawn troops to Europe. More than 3,000 troops are in Iraq, and U.S. and coalition forces have conducted more than 1,000 air strikes to fight ISIS in Iraq and Syria. The troop presence in Afghanistan, while absent from the headlines in recent years, continues. In Liberia, 2,300 troops are helping to contain the Ebola epidemic.

It is difficult, however, to reconcile policy makers' inclination to employ the military as a bulwark against all manner of threats with their inaction on the crippling spending cuts of the past several years. The defense budget can only impact the state of the military, not when policy makers call upon it for the next mission. As demonstrated in recent years, cutting the military budget does not necessarily mean the military will do less.

Matching resources to missions for the Department of Defense (DOD) is further complicated by the unique military "can-do" ethos. In other words, even if the military is not fully prepared for a particular mission, they will still undertake that mission if ordered by the president.

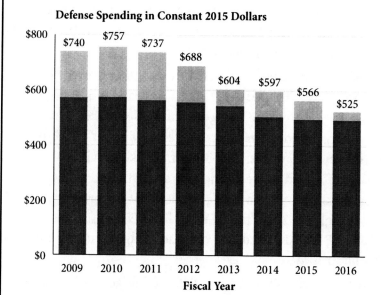

Total Defense Budget Facing 31 Percent Cut from 2010 to 2016

Defense Spending in Constant 2015 Dollars

Base spending

Overseas Contingency Operations (OCO)

Note: The 2016 figure is comprised of Budget Control Act levels of spending for the base budget and Defense Department estimates for Overseas Contingency Operations. Source: U.S. Department of Defense, *National Defense Budget Estimates for FY 2015*, April 2014, http://comptroller.defense.gov/Portals/45/Documents/defbudget/fy2015/FY15_Green_Book.pdf (accessed January 16, 2015).

TAKEN FROM: Diem Nguyen Salmon, "A Proposal for the FY 2016 Defense Budget," Heritage Foundation, January 30, 2015.

When the military is called upon to act, but constrained in its means, it runs greater risks in the endeavor. In conflict, greater risk can mean higher casualty rates or outright failure to complete the mission. If the military is ordered to war without a proper consideration of resources, that risk will be absorbed by the men and women in uniform.

Budgets and the state of the military do not dictate operational tempo. Those are dictated by external factors and by the Commander in Chief and Congress. Given their reliance on the military, it is incumbent on these stakeholders to reverse the spending cuts that increase the risks to the military and threaten its ability to execute.

Defense cuts have occurred in three phases over six years. The first phase (FY 2010–FY 2011) incurred a $20 billion reduction in the top line and concentrated cuts on terminating or reducing modernization programs. The FY 2012 budget was then cut by another $49 billion. Unlike previous years, the cuts were focused on reducing end strength and finding internal savings, rather than axing modernization programs. Halfway through FY 2013, the BCA and the Bipartisan Budget Act of 2013 (BBA) dictated the defense budget, cutting another $38 billion to date.

In total, since FY 2010, the defense budget, including overseas contingency operations (OCO) spending, has been cut 25 percent in inflation-adjusted dollars.

FY 2010 and FY 2011

While the FY 2010 budget slightly increased the defense budget, the department began cancelling major programs that year. For the FY 2010 budget, the department announced:

- Cancellation of the F-22 Raptor fighter aircraft;

- Cancellation of the VH-71 presidential helicopter;

- Cancellation of the vehicle portion of the Future Combat System;

- Cancellation of missile defense programs, including the Airborne Laser and the Multiple Kill Vehicle;

- Cancellation of the CSAR-X search and rescue helicopter; and

- The end of C-17 Globemaster III military transport production at 205 aircraft.

In FY 2011, the cuts focused on modernization spending:

- Ending C-17 production at 223. (Congress blocked the first attempt.)

- Cancelling the F-35 alternate engine program.

- Cancelling the CG(X) future large cruiser.

- Cancelling the Navy's EP-X future intelligence aircraft.

In some cases, these cuts were necessary because the program requirements were not a high priority or because the program was too costly. On the other hand, other cancellations have led to serious problems for the military today. For example, cancellation of the next-generation cruiser will lead to a future shortfall in large surface combatants for the Navy. The Navy is trying to limit the severity of the future shortfall by laying up half of the existing cruisers, thereby extending the life of half of the ships. Meanwhile, the termination of the F-22 program, which was deemed too costly, has left the Air Force with 26-year-old F-15s and no replacement plans. The Air Force's ability to conduct air superiority missions is now at risk.

FY 2012

The FY 2012 budget request cut $78 billion from the previous year's Future Years Defense Program (FYDP) for FY 2012–FY 2016. Secretary Robert Gates proposed $178 billion in savings, of which $100 billion would be reinvested into the budget. The savings came from:

- Reducing the Army and Marine Corps end strengths;

- Freezing civilian workforce levels and pay;

- Closing the Joint Forces Command;

- Reducing reports, studies, boards, and commissions;

- Reorganizing staff in each service;

- Improving business practices; and

- Cancelling or reducing additional programs, including the Marine Corps's Expeditionary Fighting Vehicle (EFV) and the Surface-Launched Advanced Medium-Range Air-to-Air Missile (SLAMRAAM).

FY 2013

The FY 2013 budget request under Secretary Leon Panetta continued the military drawdown. The FY 2013 request was $30 billion lower than the FY 2012 budget, and $259 billion was cut from the FYDP. As in previous years, the military found "savings" of $61 billion, which was cut from the budget rather than reinvested. Examples of such savings were limiting civilian pay raises to 0.5 percent and delaying facility construction projects. In the end, however, the proposed FY 2013 budget was irrelevant. In March 2013, sequestration took effect, negating Secretary Panetta's drawdown plan.

The 2013 sequestration cut $37.2 billion (6 percent) from the FY 2013 budget. The sequestration was applied by automatically cutting all programs with the exception of military personnel spending. The implementation resulted in an 8.9 percent cut to procurement, an 8.7 percent cut to research and development, and a 7.4 percent cut to operation and maintenance. These were cuts in military readiness from which the DOD is still trying to recover today.

FY 2014 and FY 2015

The BBA provided limited relief from the BCA's discretionary top lines for FY 2014 and FY 2015, but the defense budget was still far lower than previous plans. Once again, the department made cuts. Most recently, the FY 2015 budget proposed:

- Reducing the Army end strength to 420,000 and Marine Corps end strength to 175,000;

- Retiring one aircraft carrier early, reducing the carrier force to 10;

- Laying up 11 of the 22 cruisers;

- Retiring aircraft, such as the A-10 Thunderbolt II close air support aircraft; and

- Reducing purchases for many modernization programs.

In sum, the past six years of defense cuts have severely degraded the military. It is now smaller, less capable, and ill prepared for future requirements. Meanwhile, the world has become more tumultuous, increasing the demands on the military.

Supporters of Defense Cuts Are Misguided

Some argue that the spending reductions were not a problem because of the sheer size of the budget and excessive waste in the department. This is a misperception of the DOD budget. While waste does affect the DOD budget, it comprises a small portion of the overall budget, not nearly equivalent to the amount that was cut. To illustrate this, in the "Department of Everything" former Senator Tom Coburn (R-OK) itemizes an expansive list of wasteful programs in the DOD amounting to $67.9 billion over 10 years. If Congress could eliminate every single one of the listed programs, the annual savings would amount to a little more than 1 percent of the budget.

It is also wrong to assume that simply reducing overall defense spending can eliminate waste. In truth, eliminating wasteful spending at the DOD (as in other government institutions) requires separate legislation and internal reform. The past several years of defense spending reduction not only cut the fat, but also much of the actual meat—real U.S. military capabilities.

Another argument in favor of recent defense cuts claims that the department has benefitted from earlier budget growth and that these cuts are just a natural drawdown. . . . Defense spending is historically cyclical. Increases in spending tend to be linked to periods of war or conflict and are immediately followed by reductions, as in the past decade, when spending grew after the September 11, 2001, terrorist attacks and the start of the global war on terrorism.

However, the post-2001 budget growth cannot be used to justify recent cuts. First, the initial growth was largely invested in capabilities needed specifically to fight Operation Iraqi Freedom and Operation Enduring Freedom [that is the wars in Iraq and Afghanistan], namely end strength and equipment for the Army, such as mine resistant ambush protected (MRAP) vehicles and HMMWVs (Humvees [or high mobility multipurpose wheeled vehicles]). These investments do not necessarily translate into capabilities that may be needed for future military engagements. Second, the defense spending reductions began while military troops were still engaged in hostilities.

> *"Taking cuts out of the hands of Congress is the only, repeat 'only' way to cut waste from our trillion dollar defense/militarism spending."*

Sequestration: The Way to Cut Defense Waste

Jon Basil Utley

Jon Basil Utley is associate publisher of the American Conservative. *In the following viewpoint, he argues that sequestration, which put in place automatic defense cuts as part of an act to reduce budget spending, is a good thing. Utley says that defense spending is too high but that Congress refuses to make cuts on its own because of interest group pressure. Sequestration will force reevaluation of military pay and benefits, weapons systems, and base closings. Utley concludes that such reconsideration is vital if military spending is to be reined in.*

As you read, consider the following questions:

1. According to Utley, how much will sequestration cuts be, and how is the media misleading the public about the extent of the cuts?

2. How does Utley say health care benefits for military personnel should be cut?

3. What argument does Utley make for reducing the numbers of nuclear submarines?

Just like with base closings, taking cuts out of the hands of Congress is the only, repeat "only" way to cut waste from our trillion dollar defense/militarism spending. Reading and hearing how *The Complex*[1] screams, here are a few points about the distortions and half-truths being put out by it and by Big Government Conservatives[2]—Republican congressional leaders, neoconservatives, Heritage Foundation, *National Review*, Fox TV, *Washington Times* and the *Wall Street Journal* editorial page. Their big government program is unending wars, imperialist foreign policy, and ever expanding homeland security.

The cuts to the Pentagon budget will be only 7% or some $40+ billion, not the $500 billion they bandy about! Anyone who confuses the (unlikely) 10-year cut with next year's cut is just promoting lies. A good example is the *Wall Street Journal* editorial "*The Coming Defense Crackup*,"[3] warning that the cuts would create the smallest Navy since 1914. It intentionally confuses next year's cut with the consequences of 10-year cuts.

Ok, but when every smart bomb and missile hits its target, why does one need as many shells as the old battleships where most shots missed? During the Korean War the Air Force tried futilely for months to bomb a bridge over the Yalu River. Today destroying a bridge takes one cruise missile from a hundred miles away. In Washington we find all the big media opposed to cutting defense spending, waste and all, even the *Washington Post*. *Politico*, usually a leftist paper, publishes articles also intentionally confusing 10 years of cuts with a one-year cut. Today's congressmen can't oblige future congresses on what they will spend; defense apologists use the 10-year number to try to stop the sequestration for one year, 2013. All the big Washington newspapers are full of costly ads from defense contractors.

The money is not all for defense. At least half is for attacking other nations, as Ron Paul called it the defense/militarism[4] budget. Roughly half goes for defense, the rest is for military adventures abroad, most of them quite unnecessary, indeed counterproductive as they just create more enemies for America. Look at Turkey where 90% of the population used to support America; now 85% oppose us. Obviously if we attacked fewer foreigners we could do with much less spending. Firing 250,000[5] bullets for each dead guerilla can get expensive. As also paying $400 per gallon to get fuel to the front lines. Total defense costs are now well over a trillion dollars if one includes homeland security, nuclear bombs and off-budget stuff, e.g., $16 billion for the National Reconnaissance Office military satellites, just one of the 16 separate intelligence agencies[6].

Republican leaders claim that government spending to create jobs is a giant waste. But then they argue that such spending for military jobs is necessary to help the economy. Many openly argue that the defense budget is a jobs program[7]. Think though of how many jobs the talented, ambitious people in the defense establishment could create in the private sector. Cutting fat, not meat is the important need. But faced with even marginal cuts to the defense budget, Republicans threaten voters like big-city Democrats warning that the opposition will first cut firemen and policemen while leaving untouched all the fat, waste, pensions and welfare in city budgets. There are places we can cut without sacrificing effectiveness, and sequestration can help us find them. With that in mind, here are eight suggestions:

1. $50+ billion in free health care for anyone who served in the military for any amount of time for them and their families for the rest of their lives. Former Republi-

Sequestration and Streamlining

Still, it is true that an across-the-board sequestration of defense spending is a bad idea—it is like mowing the weeds along with the flower beds. Good projects will be cut along with bad projects. The smart thing to do is conduct oversight and cut what isn't working. The dollar goal of sequestration, though, was not the problem, just the method. Again, even with sequestration, defense spending would increase 16 percent over the next ten years compared to 23 percent without sequestration.

Streamlining defense will strengthen, not weaken, our national security. History shows that all great powers eventually get the foreign policy they can afford, not what they want. As Will Durant warned, "A great civilization is not conquered from without until it has destroyed itself within."

Tom A. Coburn,
The Debt Bomb: A Bold Plan to Stop
Washington from Bankrupting America.
Nashville, TN: Thomas Nelson, 2012, pp. 275–276.

can defense secretary [Robert] Gates recommended this cut. It's also an unfair advantage in seeking jobs over other Americans whose employers' must pay for their health care. True, America's obese and partly corrupted health care system inflates costs incredibly, but another constituency without federal subsidies would mean more votes for real reform of medical care, e.g., promoting competition in health care, obliging hospitals and doctors to post prices, stopping payoffs to doctors from Big Pharma[8], allowing nurse practitioners with databases to provide basic medical care and so on.

2. Cut 100,000 civilians out of 700,000[9] in the military held over since the Cold War, a cut suggested by former Republican navy secretary Gordon England. Instead we now have 800,000. *The Complex* loves to equate a few thousand Muslim terrorists with the giant former Soviet threat with thousands of nukes, half of Europe and a vast leftist network in America and Western Europe. The Heritage Foundation and American Enterprise Institute even argue that America should spend more now than even in Communist times.

3. Soldiers and officers now earn more than 90% of Americans with equivalent education, averaging some $50,000 yearly for enlisted men and $94,000 for officers, some 88% higher than civilians with the same education. Comparable civilian wages are far lower and without comparable benefits. See the *11th Quadrennial Review of Military Compensation* analysis on Military.com[10]. Every few years Congress passes more pay increases, even more than the Pentagon itself wants. Most military jobs are very safe nowadays; many now wear combat boots and uniforms to office jobs in the Washington suburbs. Infantry combat soldiers should maybe still retire after 20 years, but most of the military could easily work another 5 years rather than retire at 20 years and then be paid for another 40 by inflation-adjusted pensions. The retirement age was set in the 19th century.

4. Weapons manufacturing has become a source of vast corruption and overspending. Fighter planes don't need to cost some two to three hundred million dollars apiece. They do because contracts are awarded to companies in districts with influential congressmen, based on political expediency not efficiency or comparative advantage. This provides congressmen with donations

from manufacturers in their districts and builds a congressional constituency to maintain production of weapons even if later it is found to be unnecessary, unimaginably costly or even dysfunctional. Former [Ronald] Reagan navy secretary John Lehman criticized procurement in "Wasteful Defense Spending Is a Clear and Present Danger."[11]

5. The F-22 was designed in the 1980s[12] to fight now non-existent Soviet fighter planes with inputs from over 1,000 manufacturers in 44 states. The F-35's manufacturer, Lockheed Martin, now proudly advertises in Washington's *Politico* newspaper that it has 1300 suppliers in 45 states. The ad does not say that each plane is now costing some $300 million each,[13] nor that production models are sitting on runways still waiting for properly tested inputs. Some half of defense workers are unionized and contracts are often cost-plus, especially for modifications which always become necessary. The defense industry has not gone through the vast labor and middle management reforms in manufacturing which the private sector adopted. This means there is little competition among producers and many are still saddled with obsolete, unproductive union work rules. Also profits are highest in producing more aircraft carriers, tanks and fighter planes, based on World War II strategies, not for fighting guerrillas, terrorists, religious fanatics and cyber-warfare.

6. Many, many overseas bases are very superfluous and could be closed to save tens of billions. The website G2mil.com published a detailed list of suggested closings[14] to save billions, explaining why each is superfluous and how much money could be saved. Closing more bases in America could equally save more billions. Most were set up in the days of horses, buggies and then rail-

roads, when moving from one to another was slow and costly. The G2 website also published several other excellent suggestions[15] to control and improve military spending.

7. Do we really need over 50 nuclear submarines, as many as in Communist times? This subject needs vetting. The English, with just one such sub, bottled up the whole Argentine navy during the Falkland War.

8. Audit Pentagon spending—every effort to do so up to this point has failed. We just don't know all the waste and duplication. Also the GAO [Government Accountability Office] should report on the cost of using subcontractors in different congressional districts compared to the old way of producing major weapons.

The above are just a few of the ways hundreds of billions could be saved. Sequestration is the way to start. Across-the-board spending cuts are a way to force a look at all the waste and thoughtless policies.

Links

1. http://www.iraqwar.org/micomplex.htm

2. http://www.charlestoncitypaper.com/charleston/george-w-bushs-definition-of-conservatism-is-no-longer-acceptable/Content?oid=4115739

3. http://www.wsj.com/articles/SB10001424052702303567704577519103629692144

4. http://original.antiwar.com/utley/2011/03/14/call-it-the-militarism-budget/

5. http://www.washingtonpost.com/wp-dyn/content/article/2007/11/16/AR2007111600865.html

6. http://en.wikipedia.org/wiki/United_States_Intelligence_Community

7. http://www.democraticunderground.com/125158821

8. http://www.washingtonpost.com/blogs/ezra-klein/wp/2012/07/20/weve-spent-billions-on-lethal-pricey-medicare-drugs-can-obamacare-do-better/

9. http://www.nytimes.com/2011/07/15/opinion/15England.html?_r=0

10. http://www.military.com/warfighters

11. http://www.wsj.com/articles/SB124787043032160493

12. http://www.globalsecurity.org/military/systems/aircraft/f-22-history.htm

13. http://www.wired.com/2011/12/f-22-real-cost/

14. http://g2mil.com/OBCL.htm

15. http://g2mil.com/FY2010.htm

> "Another year of sequestration would bring chaos, waste, and lasting disruption."

Sequestration Is a Poor Way to Approach US Military Cuts

Cindy Williams

Cindy Williams is a principal research scientist of the security studies program at Massachusetts Institute of Technology. In the following viewpoint, she argues that the sequestration cuts, which impose automatic reductions on defense spending, cause chaos and are not strategically targeted. She says that the cuts are likely to remain in place, reducing defense spending year after year, and that defense officials and Congress must work together to make sure reductions are logical and fit into strategic planning. In particular, she argues that pay and health benefits could be reduced substantially, since both have grown out of control. She says this would leave resources for a careful rethinking of military goals.

As you read, consider the following questions:

1. According to Williams, what could the president and the Department of Defense have done differently to mitigate the effects of the sequestration cuts?

2. Why does Williams say that the Budget Control Act (BCA), or sequestration, is not going away?

3. Why are medical health care costs growing so quickly, according to Williams?

On March 1, 2013, the U.S. Department of Defense lost $37 billion overnight to sequestration. The cut marked the first wave of a series of planned cutbacks that will shrink future budgets across the federal government by about $1 trillion over nine years. The reductions had been set in motion back in 2011, when a special "super committee" established by the Budget Control Act (BCA) failed to reach a deficit-reduction agreement, triggering automatic cuts designed to punish both parties. Unlike other budget cuts, sequestration is implemented across the board, taking the same percentage bite out of every account. Except for the decision to spare the military personnel account that provides the pay for the United States' men and women in uniform, defense leaders had no choice about where to take the 2013 cuts. And so, with just seven months left in the fiscal year, sequestration abruptly erased about eight percent of the Pentagon's budget for the year.

Chaotic Cuts

Not surprisingly, sequestration has infuriated defense officials. On August 1, 2013, with the start of the 2014 fiscal year just two months away, Ashton Carter, the deputy secretary of defense, and James Winnefeld, the vice chairman of the Joint Chiefs of Staff, testified that another year of sequestration would bring chaos, waste, and lasting disruption.

It didn't have to be this way. President Barack Obama signed the BCA in August 2011. By the end of the year, the super committee established to craft a fiscal bargain that would replace the nine-year automatic budget cuts embedded in the bill had crashed and burned, triggering the nine-year budget cuts that began with the March 2013 sequestration. So the White House and the Department of Defense have had two years to develop a national security strategy consistent with the new budget limits, design forces and programs to match that strategy, point the Pentagon down a somewhat less abrupt budgetary glide path, and institute measures to smooth the downsizing. Instead of doing any of these things, the Obama administration and the Department of Defense have played a protracted game of chicken with Congress. All that time was wasted.

What's worse, officials seem to have learned nothing from their failures. Instead of crafting their own coherent plan to absorb the required cuts, they will again sit by and let the arbitrary sequestration machine make their decisions for them. For 2014, the BCA requires a reduced defense budget, but it allows policy makers to choose what to cut; it does not demand that every defense account be cut by the same percentage through sequestration. Rather, it calls for sequestering only the part of the appropriated defense budget that exceeds the BCA's cap. If the Pentagon had submitted a budget consistent with that limit, and if Congress had appropriated that amount, there would be no sequestration for 2014. But defense officials chose not to comply with the cap, and Congress, as of September 2013, looks poised to appropriate more than its own budget-control law allows. If that happens, the Pentagon will be in for a second round of mechanical cuts.

Still, defense leaders naively dream that the president and Congress can find an alternative. In the summer of 2013, the Pentagon finally unveiled the findings of its Strategic Choices and Management Review (SCMR), which considered how it might deal with a smaller budget. But as Carter's accompanying testimony revealed, the department, rather than embrace a smaller budget, continues to act as though it can avert the cuts entirely, or at least delay them, if it just explains how disruptive they will be. "We hope we will never have to make the most difficult choices that would be required if the sequestration-level budgetary caps persist," Carter said. "Strategic cuts are only possible if they are 'back-loaded,'" he added—in other words, put off for years.

But the BCA is not going away. Cutting defense may be nobody's first choice for dealing with the government's fiscal problems, but it is also no politician's last choice. As much as Republicans hate military cuts, they hate raising taxes even more. And as much as Democrats don't want to look stingy with security, they are even more afraid to skimp on Social Security or Medicare. Moreover, the political costs of keeping the BCA in place are low: Since the law is already on the books, no politician has to vote again for the cuts. Add fiscal considerations to those political realities, and the chances of turning back the clock on the BCA look even slimmer: With the exception of a few years during and after World War II, U.S. federal debt now composes a larger share of the economy than ever before. Given that reality, even if the law were ultimately overturned, any grand bargain between Republicans and Democrats would surely include defense cuts at least as large as those the Pentagon now faces.

American defense planners therefore need to accept the obvious: Budget cuts are here to stay. The time to plan for cutbacks and start reshaping the military was two years ago, when the writing was already on the wall. Since that never happened, the government must catch up fast. Congress, for its part, should allow the Pentagon to control its mounting personnel costs. The Pentagon and the White House, meanwhile, should come up with a national security strategy that the country can actually afford, reshaping U.S. forces to reflect that strategy and preserve the best military in the world.

Personnel Development

For the 2014 fiscal year, the BCA reduces the nonwar defense budget by about ten percent compared with the plan the president submitted to Congress in April 2013—returning it, in real terms, close to its 2007 level and holding it about there until 2021. But the Pentagon cannot buy the forces it had in 2007 with the budget it had in 2007, because several categories of spending are growing faster than inflation. Prominent among these are military health care and military and civilian pay—massive costs that the government must start getting under control now.

Between 1998 and 2013, military pay rose by more than 60 percent in real terms. The pay of the nearly 800,000 civilian workers employed by the Department of Defense rose by nearly as much. During that same period, the costs of health care for military personnel and retirees and their families and survivors more than doubled in real terms. Absent policy changes, those costs will continue to outstrip inflation by wide margins over the coming decade. Pay and medical costs will take increasingly big bites out of military capability.

Initially, the Pentagon supported the rise in pay as a way to improve recruiting and retention, which it had difficulty with in the late 1990s. The military also worried that its raises had underperformed the private sector's for about 15 years. Consistent with those concerns, Congress required that annual pay raises for military personnel and federal civilian employees exceed wage growth in the private sector until 2006.

By 2007, annual increases in pay and allowances had more than made up for the relatively lower raises of earlier years, and the Pentagon began asking Congress for more modest annual raises. Under pressure from military and veterans' associations and fearful of stinting the military in a time of war, however, Congress persistently added more than the department requested. The result is that today's military officers take more home in their paychecks than eight out of ten college-educated civilians. In terms of their income, enlisted members most resemble the 90th percentile of civilians with comparable levels of education and experience.

Medical Costs

The Pentagon's medical costs are also on the rise, and not just because the underlying costs of health care in the United States have grown. The Pentagon adopted its current health plan, called Tricare, in the mid-1990s. It set the fees that retirees would pay to use the system yet made no provisions for adjusting those fees as medical costs rose. As a result, the share of health care costs borne by military retirees using the plan dropped over the years, even as the premiums and co-pays they would have paid through their post-military employers skyrocketed. The upshot is that most military retirees now choose Tricare, and the costs to the government show it.

Since 2006, the Defense Department has asked repeatedly for permission to raise health insurance fees on military retirees. Changing the cost-sharing arrangement would of course help defray the government's costs, but more important, it would also make the government's insurance plan less attractive to retirees who have other good health coverage options. Yet Congress, under the same pressure it has faced about pay, has turned down all but the tiniest rise in fees.

The SCMR suggested new mechanisms to get military retirees to use private sector insurance if it is available to them, and changes like this make a lot of sense. After 15 years of expansion in their pay and benefits, service members, civilian Defense Department employees, and military retirees are financially well rewarded for their dedication and sacrifice. Moreover, with the war in Afghanistan drawing to a close and jobless rates still above seven percent in the private sector, recruiting and retention remain strong.

As long as defense budgets overall kept growing year after year, it was easy for Congress to turn down the Pentagon's requests to tap the brakes on pay and benefits. Now, however, with wars ending and budgets shrinking so abruptly, lawmakers might finally agree to the department's recommendations. Doing so would save an average of tens of billions of dollars each year over the coming decade, enough to spare three Army brigades, 30 Navy ships, and four Air Force squadrons from the chopping block.

Selecting a Strategy

The White House and the Pentagon, meanwhile, need to deal with the inevitable cuts by formulating a strategy consistent with the resources the BCA provides. They last outlined a formal Defense Strategic Guidance in January 2012, which called for less emphasis on long-running stability and counterinsurgency operations in favor of greater attention to the Asia-Pacific region. Although the document laid out a somewhat less expansive global posture than had previous post–Cold War versions, it still called on the U.S. armed forces to underwrite a rules-based international order, "confront and defeat aggression anywhere in the world," and broaden already extensive military partnerships with other countries. But that strategy, as secretary of defense Chuck Hagel has admitted, is unaffordable under the BCA's funding levels.

What strategy does prove affordable will depend in part on what happens to pay and benefits. The U.S. Army and the Marine Corps already plan to cut most of the troops they added for the wars in Afghanistan and Iraq. If Congress allows a slowdown in pay raises and accepts the Pentagon's proposals to rein in the costs of military health care, then the military might need to jettison another 10 or 15 percent of its planned forces to stay within the BCA's budget limits. With forces that size, the United States might just be able to carry out a less ambitious version of the strategy of rebalancing toward Asia that officials articulated in January 2012.

If, on the other hand, Congress continues to prevent the pay and benefits changes the Pentagon wants, then the military will have to shrink after only a few years of the BCA's limits by as much as 25 percent from the size it now hopes to retain. At that level, a far more restrained strategy will be needed: one that gives up on trying to reform the rest of the world's governments in favor of protecting a narrower range of U.S. national security interests, including the country's safety, sovereignty, territorial integrity, and relative power position. Restraint would mean going to war only when narrowly defined security interests were at stake and having allies provide for more of their own security. This strategy may not be the one Obama officials prefer, but it is the strategy that will be forced on them unless they can come to an agreement with Congress to avert the mandatory cuts.

> "Deep cuts in defense expenditures will impair our national security, cripple a vital part of the manufacturing sector, and have far-reaching negative effects on a broad spectrum of the U.S. economy."

Defense Spending Cuts Will Destroy Jobs

National Association of Manufacturers

The National Association of Manufacturers (NAM) is the nation's largest manufacturing industrial trade association. In the following viewpoint, NAM argues that cuts in defense spending will create job losses, both in the manufacturing sector and throughout the economy. It suggests that cuts in defense will also threaten American security and concludes that Congress should not reduce the defense budget.

As you read, consider the following questions:

1. According to NAM, how many jobs will be lost in 2014 because of sequestration defense cuts?

2. According to the viewpoint, what are the ten states most affected by job losses from defense cuts?

National Association of Manufacturers, "Defense Spending Cuts: The Impact on Economic Activity and Jobs," April 2012. Courtesy of US House of Representatives.

3. Which manufacturing sectors will experience the greatest job losses, according to NAM?

Dramatic cuts in defense spending under the Budget Control Act of 2011 (BCA) will have a significant, negative impact on U.S. jobs and economic growth. A new report, "Defense Spending Cuts: The Impact on Economic [Activity] and Jobs," looks at the combined impact of the BCA budget caps and the law's across-the-board cuts under sequestration. The report concludes that:

- 1,010,000 private sector jobs, including 130,000 manufacturing jobs, will be lost in 2014.

- GDP [gross domestic product] will be almost 1 percent lower by 2014.

- Total job losses will increase the unemployment rate by 0.7 percent.

- California will experience the largest job losses in 2014 (148,000), followed by Virginia (115,000) and Texas (109,000).

- Certain industries will be hit particularly hard, with the aerospace industry losing 3.4 percent of its jobs, the ship and boat industry losing 3.3 percent of its jobs and the search and navigation industry losing 9.3 percent of its jobs.

Negative Impact on Economic Growth

Under the budget caps and sequestration, real defense expenditures will decline progressively from 2012. The report finds that, compared to the status quo, real defense spending will be 9 percent lower in 2015 and almost 11 percent lower by 2022. The impact of these cuts will have a negative impact on economic growth, especially in the short run. By 2014, GDP will be almost 1 percent lower with both the budget caps and sequestration.

Based on the findings in the report, peak job loss will occur in 2014, with the spending cuts from the budget caps and sequestration costing the U.S. economy 1,010,000 private sector jobs, including 130,000 manufacturing jobs. With the additional loss of over 200,000 military jobs in 2014, including civilian workers, the total loss will be over 1.2 million jobs, and the unemployment rate will increase by 0.7 percent.

The impact on employment from cuts in defense spending includes both the loss of jobs at defense contractors due to a decrease in purchases for equipment, supplies and services, as well as the additional job loss at the firms that supply the direct defense contractors.

The total job numbers also reflect the impact of the "multiplier" effect across the economy since the job losses, including workers in the defense manufacturing supply chain and those employed in the military and as defense contractors, will result in lower disposable income and reduced consumer demand—creating a ripple effect across the entire economy. Despite recent growth, overall economic conditions remain weak compared to common measures of potential output and employment. Therefore, the initial multiplier effect on employment will be particularly large relative to its level under full employment.

States Suffer Further Unemployment

The report also finds that the employment impacts of the cuts in defense spending will be felt in all regions of the country.... California will experience the largest job losses (148,000), followed by Virginia (115,000) and Texas (109,000). Rounding out the top 10 are Florida, New York, Maryland, Georgia, Illinois, Pennsylvania and North Carolina.

While job losses will spread among a wide range of manufacturing industries, many of these jobs tend to be at the direct and indirect suppliers of defense equipment and supplies.

Manufacturing Is Critical to Our National Defense

We need to be able to produce the goods that allow us to defend America. American manufacturers supply the military with essentials, including tanks, fighter jets, submarines, and other high-tech equipment. The same advances in technology that consumers take for granted support our soldiers. Kerri Houston, senior vice president for policy at the Institute for Liberty and a member of the U.S.-China Economic and Security Review Commission, writes that,

> If we are to retain our military superiority at home and abroad, we must maintain the ability to manufacture original equipment and replacement parts in the U.S. Needlessly sending defense jobs overseas will do nothing to ensure our long-term national security, which history shows will require a robust research and development, technical and manufacturing base.

In his keynote address, "Lessons for a Rapidly Changing World," at Computer Associates' CA World 2003 conference, former secretary of state Henry Kissinger said, "The question really is whether America can remain a great power or a dominant power if it becomes primarily a service economy, and I doubt that. I think that a country has to have a major industrial base in order to play a significant role in the world. And I am concerned from that point of view."

Michele Nash-Hoff,
Can American Manufacturing Be Saved?:
Why We Should and How We Can.
Washington, DC: Coalition for a Prosperous America, 2012.

The largest job losses will be in the large nondurables (food, textiles, chemicals and fuels) and transport equipment sectors.

The biggest proportional reductions will be within transportation equipment and instruments:

- Aerospace (3.4 percent by 2015, 2.3 percent by 2022)

- Ships and boats (3.3 percent by 2014, 1.7 percent by 2022)

- Search and navigation equipment (9.3 percent by 2016, 8.6 percent by 2022)

Related industries will also be impacted. Across the various service sectors, the maximum loss will be 1.0 percent or less. However, since these tend to be large employment sectors, this loss results in large absolute numbers of unemployed. The biggest losers in terms of job numbers in 2014 will be as follows:

- Wholesale and retail trade (226,000)

- Business services (182,000)

- Other services (157,000)

Business services, which include professional and computer programming services, and transportation services will lose many jobs through lower defense expenditures. By 2014, the peak year of total job losses, employment will be down about 0.3 to 0.4 percent in agriculture and mining, and construction employment will be reduced by 1.5 percent.

Manufacturing Jobs on the Chopping Block

The National Association of Manufacturers (NAM) has long recognized the importance of the defense sector to our nation's innovation and economy. More than 115 years ago, the NAM was founded to promote trade and national defense. This commitment continues today. Manufacturers support important policies that promote the defense and aerospace industries and the broader manufacturing sector. Supporting them will help lift the entire economy.

In discussing programmatic changes to the defense sector during the current effort to address our nation's fiscal challenges, it is critically important that policy makers understand that deep cuts in defense expenditures will impair our national security, cripple a vital part of the manufacturing sector and have far-reaching negative effects on a broad spectrum of the U.S. economy.... Potentially deep cuts in defense procurement will have a massive ripple effect throughout the manufacturing economy, affecting large defense contractors, tens of thousands of small- and medium-sized manufacturers in the defense supply chains and over 1 million workers throughout the United States. It is critical that policy makers take action as soon as possible to avoid these negative impacts on our manufacturing sector and our economy as a whole.

"Having a giant undercover military jobs program is an insane way to keep Americans employed."

Defense Spending Is a Terrible Way to Try to Create Jobs

Robert B. Reich

Robert B. Reich is a professor of public policy at the University of California, Berkeley, and he was the secretary of labor in the Bill Clinton administration. In the following viewpoint, he argues that defense spending is often a covert jobs program. Congress often refuses to cut defense programs, even at the Defense Department's request, because the programs create jobs. He argues, however, that a jobs program for building weapons that America doesn't need is wasteful and a poor use of resources. He believes the government should invest and create jobs in areas where the United States actually needs improvement, such as in education or infrastructure.

As you read, consider the following questions:

1. Why did earnings rise in San Antonio, Texas; Virginia Beach, Virginia; and Washington, DC, when they fell in the rest of the country, according to Reich?

2. Name two programs that Reich says Robert Gates wanted to cut, though Congress wouldn't let him.

3. What two jobs programs does Reich say were justified by national defense?

America's biggest—and only major—jobs program is the U.S. military.

Covert Jobs Program

Over 1,400,000 Americans are now on active duty; another 833,000 are in the reserves, many full time. Another 1,600,000 Americans work in companies that supply the military with everything from weapons to utensils. (I'm not even including all the foreign contractors employing non-U.S. citizens.)

If we didn't have this giant military jobs program, the U.S. unemployment rate would be over 11.5 percent today instead of 9.5 percent.

And without our military jobs program personal incomes would be dropping faster. The Commerce Department reported Monday [in August 2010], the only major metro areas where both net earnings and personal incomes rose last year were San Antonio, Texas; Virginia Beach, Virginia; and Washington, D.C.—because all three have high concentrations of military and federal jobs.

This isn't an argument for more military spending. Just the opposite. Having a giant undercover military jobs program is an insane way to keep Americans employed. It creates jobs we don't need but we keep anyway because there's no honest alternative. We don't have an overt jobs program based on what's really needed.

For example, when Defense Secretary Robert Gates announced Monday his plan to cut spending on military contractors by more than a quarter over three years, congressional leaders balked. Military contractors are major sources of jobs back in members' states and districts. California's Howard P.

"Buck" McKeon, the top Republican on the House Armed Services Committee, demanded that the move "not weaken the nation's defense." That's Congress-speak for "over my dead body."

Gates simultaneously announced closing the Joint Forces Command in Norfolk, Virginia, that employs 6,324 people and relies on 3,300 private contractors. This prompted Virginia Democratic senator Jim Webb, a member of the Senate Armed Services Committee, to warn that the closure "would be a step backward." Translated: "No chance in hell."

Gates can't even end useless weapons programs. That's because they're covert jobs programs that employ thousands.

He wants to stop production of the C-17 cargo jet he says is no longer needed. But it keeps 4,000 people working at Boeing's Long Beach assembly plant and 30,000 others at Boeing suppliers strategically located in 40 states. So despite Gates's protests the Senate has approved ten new orders.

That's still not enough to keep all those C-17 workers employed, so the Pentagon and Boeing have been hunting for foreign purchasers. The Indian Air Force is now negotiating to buy ten, and talks are under way with several other nations, including Oman and Saudi Arabia.

Ever wonder why military equipment is one of America's biggest exports? It's our giant military jobs program in action.

Gates has also been trying to stop production of a duplicate engine for the F-35 Joint Strike Fighter jet. He says it isn't needed and doesn't justify the $2.9 billion slated merely to develop it.

But the unnecessary duplicate engine would bring thousands of jobs to Indiana and Ohio. Cunningly, its potential manufacturers, Rolls-Royce and General Electric, created a media blitz (mostly aimed at Washington, D.C., where lawmakers would see it) featuring an engine worker wearing a "Support Our Troops" T-shirt and arguing the duplicate engine will create 4,000 American jobs. Presto. Despite a veto threat from the White House, a House panel has just approved funding the duplicate.

By the way, Gates isn't trying to cut the overall Pentagon budget. He just wants to trim certain programs to make room for more military spending with a higher priority.

The Pentagon's budget—and its giant undercover jobs program—keeps expanding. The president has asked Congress to hike total defense spending next year 2.2 percent, to $708 billion. That's 6.1 percent higher than peak defense spending during the [George W.] Bush administration.

This sum doesn't even include homeland security, veterans affairs, nuclear weapons management, and intelligence. Add these, and next year's national security budget totals about $950 billion.

That's a major chunk of the entire federal budget. But most deficit hawks don't dare cut it. National security is sacrosanct.

Yet what's really sacrosanct is the giant jobs program that's justified by national security. National security is a cover for job security.

This is nuts.

Create Things We Need

Wouldn't it be better to have a jobs program that created things we really need—like light-rail trains, better school facilities, public parks, water and sewer systems, and non-carbon energy sources—than things we don't, like obsolete weapons systems?

Historically some of America's biggest jobs programs that were critical to the nation's future have been justified by national defense, although they've borne almost no relation to it. The National Defense Education Act of the late 1950s trained a generation of math and science teachers. The National [Interstate and] Defense Highways Act created millions of construction jobs turning the nation's two-lane highways into four- and six-lane interstates.

Maybe this is the way to convince Republicans and blue-dog Democrats to spend more federal dollars putting Americans back [to work], and working on things we genuinely need: Call it the National Defense Full Employment Act.

Periodical and Internet Sources Bibliography

The following articles have been selected to supplement the diverse views presented in this chapter.

David Adesnik	"A Strong Defense Is No Luxury," *U.S. News & World Report*, February 27, 2015.
Robert J. Barro and Veronique de Rugy	"Defense Spending and the Economy," Mercatus Center, May 7, 2013.
Dan Froomkin	"US Military Spending Still Up 45% over Pre-9/11 Levels; More than Next 7 Countries Combined," *The Intercept*, April 20, 2015.
John McCain and Mac Thornberry	"America's Dangerous Defense Cuts," *Wall Street Journal*, March 9, 2015.
Lindsey Neas	"Sequestration Has Dramatically Reduced the US Military's Combat Readiness," *St. Paul Pioneer Press* (Minnesota), April 27, 2015.
Andy O'Brien	"America's Excessive Military Spending," *Mississippi Collegian*, April 16, 2015.
David Rogers	"Hawks Face Big Obstacle on Defense Spending: President Obama," *POLITICO*, March 31, 2015.
Veronique de Rugy	"Republicans: The Cocaine Monkeys of Defense Spending," The Daily Beast, April 8, 2015.
Rebecca Shabad	"US Military Spending Drops as Other Regions Boost Defenses," *The Hill*, April 13, 2015.
Leo Shane III	"Defense Cuts Spark Worries About Troops' Careers, Pay," *Military Times*, February 25, 2015.
Travis J. Tritten	"Congress Passes Defense Budget with Troop Benefit Cuts," *Stars and Stripes*, December 12, 2014.

OPPOSING
VIEWPOINTS®
SERIES

CHAPTER 2

In What Conflicts Should the United States Intervene?

Chapter Preface

In March 2014, the Middle Eastern nation of Yemen descended into civil war, with Muslim Shiite rebels against the Muslim Sunni majority. The Shiites have received encouragement and support from Iran; the Sunnis have received backing from Saudi Arabia.

The United States is an ally of Saudi Arabia and a wary enemy of Iran. It has long-term ties to Yemen as well. As a result, US officials decided to become involved in the conflict. "There was no prime-time address by the president or secretary of defense—the only two people in the national command authority who can lawfully direct the U.S. military to engage in hostilities," Micah Zenko wrote in *Foreign Policy* in March 2015. "Yet, make no mistake, the United States is a combatant in this intervention." Zenko pointed out that the United States is providing intelligence to help Saudi Arabia bomb rebels and is providing aerial refueling for Saudi aircraft.

The justification for intervention in Yemen has varied. The administration has said it is trying to protect Saudi Arabia's borders, while Senator Richard Burr declared that the United States "can't allow Iran to take a foothold in Yemen." Other members of Congress have said that the civil war in Yemen threatens regional stability.

A number of commenters have argued that the US intervention is misguided. Andy Freeman, for example, a columnist at the *Collegiate Times*, argued in a May 2015 article that the US blockade of Yemen merely antagonized Iran, adding that "the United States has nothing to gain from reinstalling the Sunni government, and though some claim it will restore order and deny terrorist groups a safe haven, it is a fact that various groups already utilized the uncontrolled territories of the country." Ivan Eland, director of the Center on Peace and

Liberty, argued that the US bombing campaign in Yemen has not defeated the rebels "but has increased chaos and suffering in the country." He warned that this may create sympathy and support for the Sunni terrorist group al Qaeda in the Arabian Peninsula, a group that has tried to launch terrorist attacks on the United States.

The viewpoints included in this chapter debate the pros and cons of US intervention in other conflicts around the world, including in Iraq, Ukraine, and in regions where the Islamic State, or ISIS, has a strong presence.

"There is a good case for American intervention—even military—to eliminate a terrorist organization whose negotiating terms are 'capitulation or death.'"

The United States Should Adopt an Interventionist Military Policy

Gary Grappo

Gary Grappo is a former United States ambassador. In the following viewpoint, he argues that since World War II America has been committed to using its great resources and power to weed out threats and prevent humanitarian atrocities around the globe. Grappo explains that the radical terrorist group the Islamic State of Iraq and Syria (ISIS), also known as the Islamic State (IS), poses a serious threat to regional stability and threatens genocide against some of Iraq's ethnic groups. Given that, Grappo says, American military intervention is justified.

As you read, consider the following questions:

1. What were the three lessons that Grappo says America learned from Pearl Harbor?

2. Which engagements justified America's post–World War II interventionist policy, according to Grappo?

3. According to Grappo, what is the humanitarian motivation for intervening against ISIS in Iraq?

Washington's decision to enter war in Iraq for the third time in a quarter century is consistent with long-held US policy.

The debate over isolationism vs. engagement is a relatively new one in American political history. No less than George Washington and John Quincy Adams warned Americans of entangling ourselves in permanent alliances and enlisting under foreign banners regardless of how seemingly righteous.

Preventing Pearl Harbor

That seemed like good advice for the young nation for well over 100 years. Then there were the two World Wars. America hesitantly entered the first, exiting with a different attitude about the world and its potential new role in it. Still, as dark clouds gathered over Europe in the 1930s and a new, more assertive power rose in Asia, few Americans were inclined to insert themselves in what was clearly a prelude to war. So resistant was the country, that for most of the period leading up to World War II, the troop levels of US armed forces were kept at dangerously low levels. Not until 1940, after the defeat of France and when all-out war appeared inevitable, did the US ramp up its army. And then there was Pearl Harbor [referring to the attack on a US naval base in Hawaii by the Japanese in 1941].

Among the many lessons America learned from its Pearl Harbor and World War II experiences were three that have become cornerstones of US foreign and national security policy. First, the US, as the only major combatant nation with its infrastructure and manufacturing base largely intact at war's end, would have to step up and play a leadership role in the world. Second, its leadership efforts must strive to attain global stability through regional and international alliances. Third, the US must be prepared to confront its enemies abroad, as opposed to at home, so as to prevent another Pearl Harbor from ever happening again.

Isolationist voices persisted, nevertheless, but the threat of communism and a nuclear-armed Soviet Union convinced the majority of Americans that their country's new role and its proactive engagement abroad were the right course. Historically speaking, however, Americans have practiced isolationism much longer than engagement. And variations of the isolationist voice persist today, for example, urging American withdrawal from the Middle East and its current turmoil, as a recent article on Fair Observer argued.

Can Washington Afford to Withdraw?

Isolationism is indeed an easier argument to make. America is flanked by two great oceans and by two stable and peace-loving democracies, Canada and Mexico—a luxury no other great power in history has had. And, of course, the US has a long list of domestic problems still unresolved. Leave the world to its problems and concentrate on fixing our own at home.

But can a nation as large as the US afford to withdraw? Or is it even possible for America to simply make itself an equal among all nations? The answer to both is simply no, not even if the US wanted to do so.

The lessons of World War II have become far more difficult in their application than in their adoption. They remain as relevant today as they were in 1945. As the lone superpower in the world, the US is the only nation that can initiate action, preferably with the support and help of other major powers, to address and help solve crises and, yes, even enforce order from time to time.

But must the US exercise a leadership role in every conflict or crisis? And what if the conflict presents little threat to US security interests but endangers the lives of hundreds of thousands of innocents? How does the US determine which crises or conflicts present a genuine threat? Does every conflict require US military force?

There is no overarching answer to such questions. International crises, conflict and discord rarely admit to simple, overarching solutions.

Since World War II, the US has gone to war on 14 occasions—from Korea through the latest wars in Afghanistan and Iraq. That does not include dispatching US troops to far-flung locales to protect or rescue Americans, defend embassies or address humanitarian crises. The American record in these is not flawless. Vietnam and Iraq stand out as two engagements in which American judgment was severely clouded, its estimate of the threat grossly exaggerated and understanding of the local political, cultural and historical context woefully inadequate. Americans paid the price for these errors—58,000 lives lost in Vietnam and 4,500 in Iraq, tens of thousands more adversely impacted by physical and psychological wounds and trillions of Americans' tax dollars spent. The toll on the countries themselves remains inestimable.

Bosnia, but Not Rwanda

Other engagements would appear to justify the post–World War II policy. Korea, the 1991 Gulf War, Bosnia in 1994–95 and Kosovo in 1999 all succeeded—with important help from NATO [North Atlantic Treaty Organization] and other allies—in halting invading forces or stopping ethnic cleansing. The 1983 Grenada invasion ended the threat to Americans living and studying there.

There have been times when the US chose not to intervene, too. It turned back Saddam Hussein's invasion of Kuwait in 1991, but merely condemned Vladimir Putin's invasion and annexation of Crimea earlier this year [in 2014]. US and NATO forces prevented ethnic cleansing in Bosnia and Kosovo, but stood by during the Khmer Rouge's 1978 genocide of nearly 2 million innocent Cambodians and the 1994 Rwandan genocide of 800,000 Tutsis. Why Bosnia but not Rwanda or Cambodia? American hands may have been clean but perhaps not their consciences.

And in the Middle East, where American policy has been challenged and criticized extensively, it has abjured military involvement in the various conflicts pitting Egypt, Jordan, Syria and the Palestinians against Israel, choosing instead to employ its no less formidable diplomatic and economic assets to address those crises. Again, the results have been mixed—Camp David in 1979 [referring to peace accords signed by Egyptian president Anwar Sadat, Israeli prime minister Menachem Begin, and US president Jimmy Carter] on the plus side, but the continuing Israeli-Palestinian conflict on the minus.

Successes do not offset failures. Rather, they call for a continuing debate and thorough reassessment of the policy and its implementation. While largely valid on the whole, the policy—exercising our unique global leadership role, pursuing global stability through alliances and confronting enemies abroad as opposed to at home—needs to be constantly evaluated. Also, the tools with which the US exercises the policy must be carefully considered.

The primary reason the US can maintain this policy is because it is the only nation that is able to bring massive—even overwhelming—resources to a conflict or crisis. These may be diplomatic, economic, logistical or technological. They must also include our military assets.

The latter tend to be more controversial, especially as applied in some regions like the Middle East. But for the policy to be truly effective, and for the US to acquire the support

ISIS Threatens the United States

Writing this in early August [2014], I have no idea how many of my Iraqi friends and brothers in arms lie fallen in battle against the invading jihadi hordes. Or they may be refugees in the humanitarian crisis involving the million Iraqis who have already fled—and the millions more who will flee if the Islamic State of Iraq and Syria (ISIS, or simply "the Islamic State," the new name for [terrorist group] al-Qaeda in Iraq) is not stopped and thrown back into the desert hell whence it emerged. This is our mutual enemy. We must recognize the existential threat that these genocidal terrorists represent to the security of the United States. If ISIS succeeds in establishing a stronghold in the ungoverned space it has violently hacked out, first from Syria and now from Iraq, then Saudi Arabia and our other regional economic and political allies will come under attack, and Europe will be next. But America is the ultimate target. ISIS leader Abu Bakr al-Baghdadi, when he was released from U.S. custody at Camp Bucca in Iraq in 2009, threatened, "I'll see you in New York."

Carter Andress, Victory Undone:
The Defeat of al-Qaeda in Iraq and Its Resurrection as ISIS.
Washington, DC: Regnery, 2014, p. xi.

and especially the respect and trust it needs to play its outsized role, it must be able to deploy its formidable military assets.

Another Round in Iraq

For the third time in a quarter century, America finds itself militarily involved in Iraq. Americans are understandably frustrated and exhausted. "Why us again?" they fairly ask. If the US reengagement in Iraq is measured against the policy sketched above, then it appears justified. First, as a global leader with the resources, we can involve ourselves and bring about a positive outcome. That is not to be discounted since there are conflicts or crises whose outcomes we cannot necessarily affect—such as Putin's annexation of Crimea.

Second, the US has been able to cobble together a coalition of more than 40 Western and Arab nations. That kind of unified force is almost indispensable in today's world to any US engagement abroad, even though Americans bear the preponderance of the burden. The symbolic and political value of such a coalition, as long as it holds, is vital. Third, the declared enemy, the Islamic State (IS), like its ideological forbear—[the terrorist organization] al Qaeda—presents a danger both to us and our allies in the region. That argues for confronting and defeating the terrorist group in Iraq and Syria before it may strike further afield in countries such as Jordan, Saudi Arabia, Turkey and Lebanon, or further destabilize Iraq.

There are other motivating factors as well. The US bears some responsibility for Iraq's current state. While the US did help establish a framework for democracy in Iraq—however fledgling it may be at present—it also inflamed deep-seated sectarian animosities. The US cannot hope to resolve those—it failed to do so after nearly nine years in Iraq—but it can help ensure that the worst elements of sectarianism, like IS, do not threaten the established order within the country or surrounding nations. Indeed, the US managed that, albeit too briefly, with the defeat of al Qaeda in Iraq in 2009 as a result of the so-called surge.

A second motivating factor is humanitarian. When the US decided to deploy its air forces to the region in September [2014], IS was poised to assault Kurdistan, whose inhabitants we had helped escape the depredations of Saddam following the first Gulf War. The US could not idly stand by and watch the tremendous advances of Kurdistan and the Kurdish people threatened. Also, IS had begun a campaign to kill or enslave the minority Yazidis of northwestern Iraq. It looked like genocide, and it was one that the US had the ability to prevent. So, Bosnia or Rwanda?

What the US cannot say at present is what happens when—though the matter of the "if" may not be entirely settled for a while—the Islamic State is defeated? Instability in Syria will remain, not to mention continuing sectarianism and division in Iraq. The US record in implanting democracies abroad is sketchy—Korea's took decades, Iraq's hangs by a thread and Vietnam's failed disastrously.

So, it would seem on the face of it, there is a good case for American intervention—even military—to eliminate a terrorist organization whose negotiating terms are "capitulation or death." What neither the US, nor any other nation involved in ousting IS has been able to articulate is: What comes next?

One should not necessarily forgo the first action—elimination of a ruthless and heedlessly violent organization threatening the lives of thousands and even millions—because of the inability to address the second. Rather, it argues for pursuit of the first and vigorous, simultaneous action to get those nations most directly involved in the conflict to answer the second question and supporting them in that effort.

"The strategy has been costly, wasteful, and counterproductive."

The United States Should Adopt a Policy of Military Restraint

Peter Dizikes

Peter Dizikes is a staff writer for MIT News, a news service of the Massachusetts Institute of Technology. In the following viewpoint, Dizikes discusses the book Restraint: A New Foundation for U.S. Grand Strategy *by Barry Posen. In the book, Posen argues that the US project of using the military to spread liberal democracy is not working. Instead, Posen contends that the United States should concentrate on particular limited strategic goals. Posen maintains that the United States is in a strong strategic position that is only weakened with needless wars with groups that do not really threaten US security.*

As you read, consider the following questions:

1. According to the viewpoint, what is the "liberal hegemony project"?

2. What are the three main international tasks that Posen says should inform the United States' grand strategy?

3. How does popular opinion view the liberal hegemony project, in Posen's view?

The ongoing turmoil in Iraq has prompted calls for a renewal of U.S. military action in that country, as well as criticism from those who want to avoid further military commitment there.

The Liberal Hegemony Project

Among the dissenters: Barry Posen, an MIT [Massachusetts Institute of Technology] political scientist who has become an increasingly vocal critic of what he sees as excessive hawkishness in U.S. foreign policy.

Posen believes that U.S. long-term strategy relies too heavily on a bipartisan commitment to military activism in order to pursue the goal of spreading liberal democracy—what he calls the "liberal hegemony project" that dominates Washington.

After years of war in Iraq and Afghanistan without lasting stability to show for it, Posen says, it is time to use U.S. military power more judiciously, with a narrower range of goals.

Liberal hegemony "has performed poorly in securing the United States over the last two decades, and given ongoing changes in the world it will perform less and less well," Posen writes in a new book, *Restraint: A New Foundation for U.S. Grand Strategy*, published this month by Cornell University Press. "The strategy has been costly, wasteful, and counterproductive."

Iraq and Afghanistan have been problematic not because of bad luck or bad decisions, Posen asserts, but because such interventions are extremely unlikely to create sustainably peaceful polities of the sort that foreign-policy activists envisioned.

"I think they're mistakes that are inherent to the [liberal hegemony] project," contends Posen, the Ford International Professor of Political Science and director of MIT's Security Studies Program.

A Three-Part Grand Strategy

In Posen's view, the U.S. has three main international tasks that should inform the country's grand strategy in foreign affairs and military deployment.

First, Posen thinks it is almost inevitable that the U.S. and other large countries will seek a geopolitical balance of power, a policy he regards as having centuries of precedent.

"Other states will balance against the largest state in the system," he says. In this view, the U.S. does need to maintain an active and well-honed military. But a theme of *Restraint* is that U.S. foreign policy starts from a position of strength, not weakness: As an economically powerful, nuclear-equipped country screened by vast oceans, Posen believes, the U.S. naturally has an extremely strong hand in international affairs, which it only weakens with wars such as the one in Iraq.

"It's very hard for anybody to generate enough power to really affect us, but it's an experiment that we've never wanted to run historically, and I don't really want to run it," says Posen—who therefore thinks the U.S. should, when necessary, act to block the rise of a hegemonic power in Eurasia.

Second, Posen believes the U.S. should be active in limiting the proliferation of nuclear weapons and in tracing their locations. Eliminating nuclear weapons altogether, he thinks, is unrealistic. However, he says, "Our mission should be to do the best we can in terms of sanctions, technology control, diplomacy, to keep proliferation slow, and to ensure, as best we can, that it's states who have nuclear weapons, and not groups who may not be deterrable."

Third, in a related point, Posen contends that the U.S. needs to be active in limiting the capabilities of terrorist

Posen's Idea of Grand Strategy

In this book [*Restraint: A New Foundation for U.S. Grand Strategy*], I offer a critique of the present grand strategy, "Liberal Hegemony," and offer the outline of an alternative, and the military strategy and force structure to support it, "Restraint." Restraint advises us to look first at the elemental strengths of the United States, which make it an easy country to defend. The United States thus has the luxury to be very discriminate in the commitments it makes and the wars it fights. . . .

The United States is a wealthy and capable state. It can afford more security than most states. But the United States has extended the boundaries of its political and military defense perimeter very far. Taken separately, each individual project has seemed reasonable and affordable, at least to its advocates. Taken together, however, they add up to an embedded system of ambitious and costly excess. For these reasons, I have signed up with the advocates of Restraint. The United States should focus on a small number of threats, and approach those threats with subtlety and moderation. It should do that because the world is resistant to heavy-handed solutions. It can do that because the United States is economically and militarily strong, well-endowed and well-defended by nature, and possessed of an enormous ability to regenerate itself. It is not smart to spend energies transforming a recalcitrant world that we could spend renewing a United States that still needs some work.

Barry R. Posen,
Restraint: A New Foundation for U.S. Grand Strategy.
Ithaca, NY: Cornell University Press, 2014.

groups, using "a mix of defensive and offensive means," as he writes in the book. At its most severe, that risk involves terrorists obtaining nuclear arms. Posen recommends a mix of intelligence and counterterrorism activities as starting points for a sustained effort to reduce the potency of terror groups.

But can a policy shift occur?

Restraint has received praise from other foreign-policy scholars. Andrew Bacevich, a political scientist at Boston University, calls it a "splendid achievement," and says that Posen "illuminates the path back toward good sense and sobriety." Richard K. Betts, of Columbia University, calls it "a realistic alternative to American overstretch."

Bipartisan Agreement

Still, Posen acknowledges that calls for more selective use of U.S. force face an uphill battle in Washington.

"The vast tracts of the American foreign policy debate are populated with people of both parties who actually agree on most things," Posen says. "They all agree on the liberal hegemony project."

He wrote the book, he says, in part to see if it were possible to craft an alternative approach in the realm of grand-strategy thinking, and then to see how much traction such a view would receive. "A coherent alternative . . . is a tool of change," Posen says. "Even if you can't win, you force the other side to think, explain, defend, and hold them to account."

Finally, Posen thinks popular opinion has turned against military interventions in a way that was not the case a decade ago, when the Iraq war was more widely regarded as a success.

"Presently public opinion is strikingly disenchanted with this grand strategy," Posen says. "There is a body politic out there that is much less hospitable to the liberal hegemony project than it's been."

Posen ascribes this less to a generalized war-weariness among the American people than to an increasing lack of public confidence in the idea that these wars have created tangible gains. Too many claims of success, he says, have created a new "credibility gap," using a phrase that originated during the Vietnam War.

"We treated [the public] to tale after tale of success, victory, progress, and none of it seems to add up, after more than a decade," Posen says. "This is interminable, and it's not credible. I think we're back in the days of the credibility gap."

> *"If Putin's aggression is not stopped in Ukraine, it will cost the West much more in lives and resources to stop him elsewhere."*

The United States Should Intervene in Ukraine

Jorge Benitez

Jorge Benitez is director of NATOSource, a news and information service, and senior fellow at the Atlantic Council. In the following viewpoint, Benitez argues that the United States and Europe could send troops to engage with Russia in Ukraine without resulting in an escalation to total war. He suggests that Russia needs to be stopped in Ukraine or Russian leader Vladimir Putin will continue to try to extend Russia's military influence and power.

As you read, consider the following questions:

1. According to Benitez, what strategy in Ukraine constitutes a defensive military option?

2. Under what circumstances, according to Benitez, could the United States attack Kaliningrad?

3. What evidence does Benitez see that Russia may attack other countries in Europe?

It is becoming harder and harder to ignore Russia's growing military intervention in Ukraine. The diplomatic and economic efforts of President Barack Obama and European leaders have failed to stop Russian president Vladimir Putin's repeated escalation of this crisis. It is irresponsible to not examine how the West can use a limited amount of force to prevent Russia from conquering more of Ukraine. No matter how reluctant transatlantic leaders are to consider military options, the simple truth is that the West can defend Ukraine from further Russian invasion and do so without a prolonged conflict.

Defensive Military Option

The key element of this military option is the important distinction that it only involves using force against Russian units attacking Ukraine. This is a defensive military option to protect Ukraine and stop Russian aggression in another country. It is not an offensive military option; only Russian forces beyond Russia's borders would be targeted. It would not be a military threat to Russia or the Russian people.

The most feasible military option to help defend Ukraine would be a combination of Western air power, special forces, intelligence, remotely powered aircraft (aka drones) and cyberpower. This limited military option requires few boots on the ground and is comparable to the options used to initially defeat larger enemy forces in Afghanistan and Libya. This will not be a NATO [North Atlantic Treaty Organization] mission, because it is improbable that all 28 members of the alliance would authorize this option. Nevertheless, a transatlantic coalition led by the U.S., Britain, France, Poland and Romania could host and deploy a more than adequate force multiplier to help the Ukrainian military defeat and repel Russian troops from their territory.

This option would require a major investment of allied air power. Russian forces in Ukraine will offer significantly more effective opposition than previous coalitions faced in Serbia, Afghanistan, Iraq and Libya. But the West does have the military capability to overcome this sophisticated adversary. In fact, Europe could defeat Russian forces without U.S. assistance if its leaders had the political will to act together and share the costs. If pooled together, Europe's national air forces have more combat planes than Russia has available west of the Urals. Even in the case of a full-scale Russian invasion of Ukraine, Putin will need to keep major portions of the Russian military protecting the border in the Far East, Central Asia, the Caucasus and the Baltic region. The combination of willing European allies with U.S. military capabilities would prove more than a match for the limited forces Putin could pour into Ukraine.

The United States and Europe Can Defeat Russia

It is necessary to acknowledge one important caveat to this option's exclusion of Russian territory from Western attacks and that is Kaliningrad, the Russian port on the Baltic. The West should initially respect Russian control over Kaliningrad. But if Russian forces from Kaliningrad or elsewhere in Russian territory use force against coalition territory or forces (including Ukraine), then Kaliningrad would lose its protection and become a legitimate target for coalition attacks.

There are some that will feel that this military option is too provocative. They will strongly oppose any direct military combat between Western forces and the Russian military. Critics will also fear that this military option will lead to even more dangerous escalation of the crisis. The political decision to use force deserves to be taken cautiously, but such caution

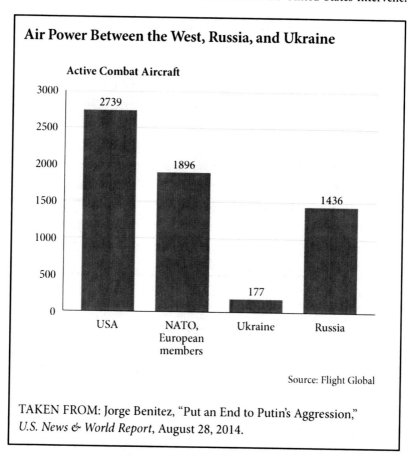

Air Power Between the West, Russia, and Ukraine

Active Combat Aircraft

Source: Flight Global

TAKEN FROM: Jorge Benitez, "Put an End to Putin's Aggression," *U.S. News & World Report*, August 28, 2014.

should not incapacitate national leaders from objectively examining the potential of a military option to do what current diplomatic and economic options have failed to do: stop Putin and save Ukraine.

We should also remember that this would not be the first time Western and Russian forces fought against each other. Moscow sent Russian air power to oppose U.N. [United Nations] and U.S. forces in Korea, and China sent hundreds of thousands of its troops to turn the tide in that conflict. By limiting combat to the Korean peninsula, the great powers clashed but collectively prevented the conflict from escalating into total war.

The use of force against Russian units attacking Ukraine does involve risk and loss of life. But so does our current policy of diplomatic condemnation and limited economic sanctions. Week after week, transatlantic leaders repeat their warnings to Putin, but he continues to escalate the crisis and the death toll in Ukraine rises.

It is highly unlikely that this military option will ever receive serious consideration from Obama and most European leaders. They prefer to communicate to Moscow that all military options are off the table for the West, even as Putin sends more Russian military hardware and personnel into Ukraine. Nevertheless, the case needs to be made for a proportional response to Putin's actions.

Putin Must Be Stopped

One of the main reasons why the West should be willing to undertake the risks and costs of this military option is that Putin will not stop after he takes what he wants from Ukraine. As he has done against Estonia, Georgia and Crimea, Putin will continue to coerce and attack his weak neighbors as long as he can do so without a strong response from the West. Will he next try to "protect" ethnic Russians in energy-rich Kazakhstan or expand Russian control beyond Transnistria to take over all of Moldova?

Or will Putin try to block the alliance choices of other neighbors? For example, Sweden and Finland are both closer to NATO membership than Ukraine. Russia's opposition to them joining NATO is almost as strong as it is to Kiev's relationship with NATO. Could Putin someday overreact to Stockholm and Helsinki's partnership with NATO and initiate another "frozen conflict" to keep Sweden and Finland out of the alliance?

Putin has communicated clearly and repeatedly that he is willing to use force to resolve disputes and that he will intervene to "protect" Russians living in neighboring countries.

Western leaders wanted to believe that the invasion of Georgia would not be repeated and that Putin would be content with Crimea. But Putin continues to defy their hopes for peace with increasing use of Russian military power. NATO leaders must ask themselves, if Putin wins militarily against Ukraine, will he stop there or will Russia be more likely to use force later against another of its neighbors?

The cyber campaigns and increased covert intelligence efforts that preceded Russia's seizure of the Crimea are already being conducted elsewhere in Europe, including within NATO members. Few observers delude themselves that Putin's emphasis on surprise 24-hour military mobilizations and exercises are being done for defensive purposes, especially after seeing the unexpected speed with which the Russian military acted against Ukraine.

If Putin's aggression is not stopped in Ukraine, it will cost the West much more in lives and resources to stop him elsewhere. No other vulnerable state along Russia's borders has the geostrategic depth and value of Ukraine. Ukraine also has the largest pro-West population to defend against Russian invasion.

The military option to save Ukraine from further Russian occupation should not be dismissed perfunctorily by Obama and European leaders. The military defense of Ukraine deserves at least a serious debate and top-level consideration.

> *"With the end of the Cold War, Ukraine is even less relevant to America's defense."*

U.S. Should Stay Out of the Russo-Ukrainian Quarrel: Why the Conflict in Ukraine Isn't America's Business, Part I

Doug Bandow

Doug Bandow is a senior fellow at the Cato Institute and a former special assistant to President Ronald Reagan. In the following viewpoint, he argues that Russia's military action in Ukraine is not a direct threat to the United States. He also says that Russia shows no signs of seeking wider territorial conquests and that Ukrainian nationalists have contributed to the conflict and have been responsible for their share of atrocities. He says, therefore, there is no moral or practical reason for American intervention. Instead, he concludes, America should work toward a diplomatic solution.

As you read, consider the following questions:

1. What six reasons does Bandow give for staying out of the Ukrainian conflict?

2. According to Bandow, what anti-American actions could Russia take if it wanted to do so?

3. What evidence does Bandow cite to show that the United States is more likely to breach the peace than Russia is?

Fighting over the Donetsk airport between Ukraine's military and separatist forces backed by Russia has flared anew. The U.S. has begun providing heavier weapons as well as personnel training to Kiev [the capital of Ukraine]. The conflict could go on for a long time, with Kiev and Moscow locked in a small hot war and the U.S. and Russia stuck in a larger Cold War lite. An extended confrontation would be in no one's interest, especially America's.

America's Promiscuous Meddling

The U.S. has made a habit of promiscuously meddling around the world. The results rarely have been pretty. Thousands of Americans have been killed, tens of thousands have been wounded, hundreds of thousands of foreigners have died, and a multitude of international furies have been loosed.

At least none of these conflicts involved a real military power. In contrast, advocates of confrontation with Russia over Ukraine want to challenge a nation armed with nuclear weapons and an improving conventional military, steeped in nationalist convictions, rooted in historic traditions, and ruled by a tough authoritarian [Russian leader Vladimir Putin]. No one should assume that in a military showdown the Kremlin would yield to Washington or that war with Moscow would be a cakewalk.

Yet Ukraine's most fervent advocates assume that any American who fails to believe that, say, inaugurating global nuclear war to save their distant ethnic homeland is a Putin troll, Russian agent, friend of dictators, proto-Communist fellow traveler, or even worse. Of course, Ukrainian nationalists are not alone in their conclusion that anyone who disagrees with them is not only wrong but evil. That's Washington politics today.

Six Reasons to Stay Out

However, the issues of the Russo-Ukraine conflict are complex with no obvious solution. People of good faith and basic intelligence can disagree about both facts and solutions. In fact, there is at least a baker's dozen of good reasons for America to stay out of today's messy, tragic, and bloody conflict involving Ukraine and Russia. The first six are reason enough: Ukraine isn't important geographically; Russia matters more than Ukraine to America; blame is widely shared for Ukraine's travails; Washington never guaranteed Ukraine's security; Vladimir Putin is not [Adolf] Hitler and Russia is not Nazi Germany (or [Joseph] Stalin's Soviet Union); and there's no genocide.

1) Ukraine isn't important geopolitically.

It might come as a shock to Kiev's strongest supporters, but Ukraine is not the center of the universe. It's obviously important to those who live there, as well as those with family or friends there. The ill humanitarian consequences of the ongoing conflict should be of concern to people of goodwill anywhere. But Ukraine is largely irrelevant to American security.

The United States was founded, developed, and became a superpower all the while Ukraine was ruled from Moscow. No one imagined that the U.S. was in any danger because that part of Eurasia was not independent. Americans were sympathetic to Ukrainians during the Cold War given the Communist regime's bloody depredations, but no one considered a campaign of military liberation. Moral offense does not mean existential threat.

With the end of the Cold War, Ukraine is even less relevant to America's defense. Russia poses no international challenge like the Soviet Union. There's no hegemonic global competition with the U.S. Moscow's relationship to Kiev is vital to Ukraine, not Washington.

Kiev's future matters more to Europe, but even that connection is limited. Europe has a population and economy bigger than that of the U.S. The continent does not need Ukraine to be prosperous or secure. The European Union hopes to keep expanding, but the European people have grown increasingly wary of bringing in poorer, more distant, and less well-governed states. Europeans understandably would prefer no instability on the continent's periphery, but Ukraine's conflict is a human tragedy, not a security threat.

Russia Is Not Challenging America

2) Russia matters more than Ukraine to America.

Moscow's policy in Ukraine is about Ukraine, not the U.S. If Russia really wanted to be America's number one enemy, as claimed by [2012 Republican presidential candidate] Mitt Romney, then Russia would have directly challenged America. It has not.

However, Moscow can cause significant trouble for Washington in a number of areas. And treating Russia as an enemy risks turning it into one. For instance, in mid-December the Putin government ended the U.S.-funded nuclear security program, which helped prevent loose nukes after the breakup of the Soviet Union. In January [2015] Russia signed an agreement with Iran for expanded defense cooperation, reportedly including long-delayed delivery of the S-300 missile air defense system. This weapon could greatly complicate plans for an American or Israeli military strike on Iran.

This might be just the start. The Putin government could arm Syria with advanced missiles, defend Tehran [the capital of Iran] against American and European pressure over its nuclear program, impede U.S. logistical operations in Afghanistan, provide advanced arms to North Korea, and transfer military technologies to China. Worse, Russia is pursuing a closer relationship with China; should that evolve into a serious anti-American axis, despite serious differences between the two states, much harm could result.

3) *Blame is widely shared for Ukraine's travails.*

Americans like their enemies to be obvious and their conflicts to be just. Alas, the Ukraine-Russia battle offers no such clarity. [Former secretary of state] Henry Kissinger recently admitted: "if the West is honest with itself, it has to admit that there were mistakes on its side." While Moscow was not justified in forcibly changing boundaries, he argued, "Ukraine has always had a special significance for Russia. It was a mistake not to realize that." Europe with America in its wake sought to dominate along Russia's border without the slightest concern over Moscow's likely reaction.

While the Putin regime's actions are unfair to Ukraine and have shocked the West, they reflect great power sensitivity to borders and demand for respect. U.S. and European leaders can forever assert that NATO poses no threat to Russia, but Moscow policy makers are not stupid. The Washington-dominated alliance was created to contain the Soviet Union and was extended up to the borders of the Soviet-successor state, Russia, after the end of the Cold War. NATO incorporated most of Moscow's former allies, which had provided a buffer to the traditional invasion route from Europe. Then Washington led NATO to dismember Serbia, an historic Russian ally.

Russia is the only serious nation against which NATO is directed. The war hawks who dominate Washington's foreign policy discourse made their designs clear. For instance, Sen. Lindsey Graham (R-SC) spoke of "creating a democratic noose around Putin's Russia," which he equated with flying "the NATO flag as strongly as I could around Putin."

Obviously the alliance did not force Moscow to act in Ukraine. But Western attempts to dominate border territories historically part of Imperial Russia as well as the Soviet Union looked particularly threatening to many Russians. Jack Matlock, former U.S. ambassador to the U.S.S.R. [Soviet Union], wrote of a "cycle of dismissive actions by the United States met by overreactions by Russia [that] has so poisoned the relationship that the sort of quiet diplomacy used to end the Cold War was impossible when the crisis in Ukraine burst upon the world's consciousness."

Worse, in Ukraine the West helped fund the "Orange Revolution" which brought to power Viktor Yushchenko, a virulent critic of Russia—which he accused (and later recanted) of trying to poison him—who wanted his nation to join NATO. The next president hailed from Ukraine's pro-Russian east, but maintained Kiev's distance from Moscow and won Russian subsidies for merely delaying his signature on a trade agreement with Europe. Then European states and America backed protestors demanding that the government accept an EU trade agreement that required painful reforms and placed Europe before Russia economically.

Next the West endorsed a sometimes violent street revolution backed by nationalists and neo-fascists against a *democratically elected* leader. Carl Gershman, head of the Washington-funded National Endowment for Democracy, called Ukraine "the biggest prize" and talked of that nation's role as a tool to oust Putin. The [Barack] Obama administration's Victoria Nuland discussed with America's ambassador to Ukraine who Washington wanted to take power in Kiev. Russians didn't have to be paranoid to view this policy as hostile to their nation's interests. Observed Ruslan Pukhov, a former Moscow defense official now with the Centre for Analysis of Strategies and Technologies: "The West underestimates the importance of the Ukrainian issue for Russia and the role of Ukraine as a colossal destabilizing factor in Western-Russian relations."

The Putin government used allied intervention as an excuse to reclaim Crimea, a territory with an ethnic-Russian majority which had been arbitrarily transferred from Russia to Ukraine in 1954. Separatist sentiment in Ukraine's east grew with Russian support but also after bloody Ukrainian attempts to reconquer the Donbas. Kiev, Brussels, and Washington share blame with Moscow for the tragic denouement in Ukraine.

No Commitment to War

4) Washington never guaranteed Ukraine's security.

Never mind whether it is in America's interest to go to war over Ukraine, argue some Kiev advocates. Washington committed itself to do so two decades ago through the 1994 Budapest Memorandums on Security Assurances after Ukraine relinquished the nuclear weapons left by the dissolution of the Soviet Union. The U.S. must "enforce" the agreement—presumably by nuclear war, if necessary.

In fact, Washington joined Britain and Russia in making a series of commitments regarding Ukraine. But none of them involved going to war. The three signatories lauded Ukraine for signing the nuclear nonproliferation treaty and committed themselves to respect Ukraine's sovereignty and borders; refrain from threatening Ukraine with military force or economic coercion; go to the UN [United Nations] on Kiev's behalf if the latter faced aggression "in which nuclear weapons are used"; refrain from using nukes against non-nuclear states; and consult "in the event a situation arises that raises a question concerning these commitments."

In short, Washington offered Ukraine no meaningful commitment to do anything practical to help Kiev in any circumstance. If the [Bill] Clinton administration had intended to defend Ukraine, the former would have presented a treaty for Senate approval or forced through Kiev's accession to NATO. But Washington was no more ready to go to war for Ukraine

Putin, Ukraine, and NATO

President [Vladimir] Putin was also allowed to attend the NATO [North Atlantic Treaty Organization] summit. In a closed meeting on April 4, 2008, he intimidated Ukraine, effectively threatening to end its existence:

- "As for Ukraine, one-third of the population are ethnic Russians. According to official census statistics, there are 17 million ethnic Russians there, out of a population of 45 million...."

- "Ukraine, in its current form, came to be in Soviet-era days.... From Russia the country obtained vast territories in what is now eastern and southern Ukraine...."

- "Crimea was simply given to Ukraine by a CPSU [Communist Party of the Soviet Union] Politburo's decision...."

- "If the NATO issue is added there, along with other problems, this may bring Ukraine to the verge of existence as a sovereign state."

In a sharp reversal of the policy of his predecessor Boris Yeltsin, Putin challenged Ukraine's legitimacy as a sovereign state and its territorial integrity. He claimed that its composition was artificial, its borders arbitrary, and the 1954 transfer of Crimea to Ukraine illegal. He ignored that Russia had guaranteed all these rights to Ukraine in half a dozen ratified international treaties. The NATO summit in Bucharest closed the road to NATO membership for Ukraine.

Anders Åslund, Ukraine:
What Went Wrong and How to Fix It. *Washington, DC:*
Peterson Institute for International Economics, 2015, pp. 77–78.

in 1994 than in 2014. Allied politicians offered high-sounding rhetoric rather than practical commitments. The Ukrainian government accepted what it could get, which was just a piece of paper.

5) *Vladimir Putin is not Hitler and Russia is not Nazi Germany (or Stalin's Soviet Union).*

World War II taught America's uber-hawks a new argument when the American people resisted their aggressive schemes: *Reductio ad Hitlerum.* Just claim that humanity faced a new Hitler and tar anyone who objected to sending in U.S. troops as an appeaser. Warn that without military action a new dark age would descend upon the globe. Over the years [Vietnam's] Ho Chi Minh, [Serbia's] Slobodan Milosevic, and [Iraq's] Saddam Hussein and a parade of other petty dictators were called the equivalent of Hitler. People who criticized proposals for war were denounced as appeasers.

Yet until 1938 and the Munich conference on Czechoslovakia appeasement was just another international tactic, well respected as a means to avoid conflict. Had the European states done a little more to appease each other in the aftermath of the June 28, 1914, assassination of the heir to the Austro-Hungarian throne [referring to Archduke Franz Ferdinand], World War I might have been avoided. And with it World War II, the continuation of the original conflict after the combatants caught their collective breath.

Even Winston Churchill admitted that appeasement was a legitimate tactic. In 1950 he declared that "the word 'appeasement' is not popular, but appeasement has its place in all policy." He also famously said that "to jaw-jaw is always better than to war-war." The problem with trying to appease Hitler was Hitler, not appeasement. The Nazi dictator simply could not be appeased, at least at a price that Western leaders ever could pay.

Vladimir Putin isn't in the same league as Hitler or Joseph Stalin. Putin is an old-style nationalist who insists that his country's interests be considered. There is no global hege-monic struggle, no grand ideological contest, no plan for widespread territorial conquest. Putin's ambitions may outrage the West, but they appear bounded. Said Kissinger of Crimea: "It was not Hitler moving into Czechoslovakia."

Indeed, if Putin hopes to reconstitute the Soviet Union, as charged by some, he's not doing very well. In power for more than 14 years, he only has gained a piece of Ukraine (Crimea), influence over two bits of Georgia (Abkhazia and South Ossetia), and contested authority over part of Ukraine (the Donbas). In the meantime, his actions have united most of his neighbors against Russia and invited imposition of debilitat-ing sanctions.

Putin is rebuilding Russia's military, but he would be a fool not to do so. Moscow has taken no action against America or vital American interests. Indeed, experience suggests that Washington is far more likely than Russia to breach the peace. Of course, U.S. officials argue that all of their interventions were justified—over the last three decades against Nicaragua, Grenada, Panama, Haiti, Bosnian Serbs, Serbia, Somalia, Af-ghanistan, Libya, Yemen, Pakistan, Syria, Iraq (recently for the third time). Russian nationalists can be forgiven for thinking differently.

No Genocide

6) There's no genocide.

America must act to stop Russia from slaughtering help-less Ukrainians, some of Kiev's most fervent advocates argue. The claim has emotional power, but is false. There have been an estimated 4800 deaths in the combat in the east. It's a tragic toll, but includes Ukrainian separatists and loyalists, and Russians. When it comes to wars, that casualty list barely counts.

Moreover, the battle for the Donbas is a typical civil war/ ethnic insurgency/secessionist movement. No one is trying to eliminate another people, characteristic of real genocide. One group is attempting to escape rule by a more distant government. The latter doesn't want to yield control. The fight is unfortunate, but no more justifies Western intervention than many similar conflicts dotting the globe.

While Moscow bears blame for intervening, the Ukrainian authorities are not blameless. The semi-violent overthrow, backed by foreign states, of the democratically elected president from the east was hardly a friendly act to those who supported him. The new regime, backed by unsavory nationalists overtly hostile to the Russian heritage of many Ukrainians, immediately targeted highly sensitive Russian language protections.

Separatist sentiments, even if manipulated by Moscow, were real, and were exacerbated by Kiev's actions. Indiscriminate bombing of rebellious cities resulted in numerous civilian deaths. Amnesty International wrote about possible war crimes by nationalist militias employed by the Ukrainian government, singling out the Aidar volunteer battalion, which acquired a "reputation for brutal reprisals, robbery, beatings and extortion." The *New York Times* reported on Kiev's *modus operandi*: "The regular army bombards separatist positions from afar, followed by chaotic, violent assaults by some of the half dozen or so paramilitary groups surrounding Donetsk who are willing to plunge into urban combat." Many refugees from the fighting have fled to Russia, rather than toward Kiev. The Ukrainian government shares the blame for the conflict's casualties.

These are reasons enough for America to stay out of the conflict. . . .

The ongoing strife in Ukraine is an unnecessary tragedy. That country's fractured and corrupt political system finally exploded into flame, fueled by a combustible mix of nationalist, ethnic, and Western influences. Years of U.S. triumphalism left many Russians suspicious and angry. After the West over-reached in a neighboring country viewed as vital by Moscow, the Putin government responded brutally. Russia is not alone in its responsibility for the ongoing conflict.

Thankfully, the battle for Ukraine doesn't much concern America. Washington should support a peaceful international order in which aggression is not the order of the day—and set its foreign policy accordingly. Americans also should demonstrate concern for the humanitarian crises in both government and rebel-held areas in Ukraine. But the U.S. has no cause to intervene, turning Russia into an enemy and militarizing a conflict not America's own.

Instead, Washington should promote a diplomatic solution, however imperfect, with which all the parties can live. The perfect outcomes preferred by the combatants must not become the enemy of a practical settlement, based on a neutral Kiev, which ends the bloodshed while leaving Ukraine free and Russia secure. The Obama administration's overriding objective should be finding a peace which may endure.

"The United States must move not just to thwart the ISIS menace, but to destroy it."

America Must Destroy ISIS

Robert W. Merry

Robert W. Merry is editor of the National Interest *and author of* A Country of Vast Designs. *In the following viewpoint, he argues that fundamentalist Islam is a grave threat to the United States, and that ISIS, the radical Islamic group in Syria and Iraq, poses a real danger to America and American interests. He concludes that the United States should do whatever is necessary to stop ISIS.*

As you read, consider the following questions:

1. What does Merry say is the difference between al Qaeda and ISIS?

2. What is the first thing Merry says President Obama should do in response to ISIS?

3. According to the viewpoint, what is Colin Powell's "Pottery Barn" rule?

Go back to the weeks and months immediately following the al Qaeda attack on the American homeland on September 11, 2001. Suppose that al Qaeda had somehow managed to become a major military power in the Middle East. Suppose further that al Qaeda had established a significant presence in Syria and conquered strategic territories in Iraq, threatening to obliterate peoples and religious sensibilities it despised. Now suppose it had set up what it called a "caliphate" to rule over that territory, demanded fealty from all Muslims everywhere and established itself as an enemy of America.

Question: Would the United States have intervened militarily to thwart this destabilizing force in the crucial Middle East and, if possible, to destroy it?

The answer is yes.

A second question: *Should* the United States have intervened in such a cause?

The answer is yes again.

That is precisely what now has happened in the Middle East—with two differences. First, it isn't al Qaeda that has forged itself into a military force that threatens to destabilize the Middle East and turn it into a hotbed of anti-Western fervor. It is, rather, an al Qaeda offshoot, the so-called Islamic State of Iraq and Syria (ISIS), a far more dangerous threat. And second, the United States, far from the coiled and angry nation that emerged after 9/11, is enervated, tired of war and tired of the Middle East.

Thus do we see a dichotomy that has President Obama in its grip. On one hand, he knows that the most powerful nation on earth has an obligation to maintain stability in crucial strategic regions of the world and also to protect its own people from real and potential threats of serious magnitude. That's why he has commenced his aerial warfare against ISIS positions in Iraq where the al Qaeda offshoot threatens to wipe out Kurdistan in the north and take Baghdad in the country's crucial central region. The whole of Iraq could soon come under the control of this Islamist force.

But, on the other hand, he knows his countrymen are extremely skittish about another Middle Eastern war that unleashes seething anti-Western passions and saps American blood and treasure. That's why he has pursued his usual approach of half-measures that make him look decisive, but have little prospect of actually changing significantly the situation on the ground, notwithstanding the initial ISIS retreat from captured territory in response to the first three days of aerial strikes.

The president knows he must do something, so he does something; but he doesn't want to do anything, so he does as little as possible.

But Obama and the country need to make some distinctions. Iraq's Saddam Hussein was not a threat to America before he was overthrown through U.S. force of arms and his country destroyed. Libya's Muammar Gaddafi was not a threat to America before he was upended with U.S. help and his country also destroyed. Syria's Bashar al-Assad was not a threat, and neither was Egypt's Hosni Mubarak, but both came under withering U.S. condemnation when weakened by internal dissent and civil war.

But ISIS represents an ominous threat to U.S. security if it is allowed to establish itself permanently as a state or quasi-state in the heart of the Middle East. It's easy to bemoan the tragic American foreign-policy folly of the past eleven years that has destabilized this crucial region and paved the way for this horrendous turn of events. But that doesn't obviate the reality that those events now pose a serious threat to regional stability and the safety of the West and America.

The seriousness of the threat calls for a cohesive and comprehensive U.S. foreign policy that takes into account the sacrifice that likely will be needed to address this crisis. A number of steps, all interrelated, should be pursued.

First, the president needs to level with the American people in a way that he has thus far avoided. He must identify Islamist radicalism as the country's primary enemy and explain why and how its rise in the Middle East would pose a serious threat to the American homeland far beyond any threat ever posed by al Qaeda. He should say that America must shoulder the burden of maintaining global stability and that it must act always in its own national interest, which begins with the protection of American sovereignty and American lives. He should abandon the nostrums of Wilsonism and concentrate on the United States' national interest. This isn't about democracy or pluralism or any kind of springtime in Arabia. It is about power and the need for America to use its power to prevent Islamist radicalism from establishing a military and geopolitical presence in the Middle East.

Second, he should clear the decks diplomatically, extricating the country from foreign controversies that lack strategic significance and serve to divert attention and resources from the immediate ISIS threat. This means negotiating an end to the unfortunate confrontation with Russia over Ukraine. It is a distraction that never made sense, but now carries too high a price. Ukraine has no strategic significance to the United States and little to Europe. It has been part of Russia's sphere of influence for 350 years. The outlines of an agreement are clear: America and the West will cease efforts to pull Ukraine into Europe and forswear any interest in getting Ukraine into NATO. Russia will accept a Western-oriented government in Kiev, so long as eastern Ukraine is granted a significant degree of cultural and governmental autonomy. Sanctions will be removed. And the two countries will explore mutual interests, including their interest in preventing a serious rise of Islamist fundamentalism. It's difficult to see how any of this would clash with vital U.S. strategic interests.

Third, the United States should pursue a diplomatic approach in the Middle East that focuses on the ISIS threat above all other considerations. That means getting tough with states—Saudi Arabia, for example, and other Sunni Gulf nations—that harbor radical elements and seem bent on exploiting the ISIS rise to thwart their Shia enemies in Iraq and Iran. It means working with countries that share U.S. concerns, including nations that have been considered adversaries in the past—Iran, for example, and Assad's Syria. The country should also make clear that it doesn't care about what kinds of governments are pursued in the countries of the Middle East or the cultural habits and sensibilities of the people there. Its only concern is the rise of Islamist radicalism.

Fourth, the United States should seek to become once again a leader of the West and operate as the core state of its civilization. Most European nations broke off from the U.S. rush to the Iraq war because they saw no merit in this Wilsonian meddling and viewed it as a destabilizing policy. They were right. But this is different, and it requires true national leadership of a Churchillian nature. All of Western civilization has a stake in the outcome of this confrontation.

Finally, once the decks have been cleared and a policy devised that is both coherent and comprehensive, the United States must move not just to thwart the ISIS menace, but to destroy it. It isn't clear what that will take, but whatever it takes must be brought to bear.

On the latest edition of *Fox News Sunday*, commentator George Will said: "Remember Colin Powell's Pottery Barn rule—if you break it, you own it. We've broken two states in the Middle East. We broke by our policies the state of Libya; we broke by our policies the state of Iraq. And we own the rubble." Host Chris Wallace asked, "So, when we own the rubble, does that mean we have the responsibility for fixing it?"

"No," replied Will, "we have a responsibility to learn the lesson at long last that we can't fix states like this."

Correct. But we have a responsibility also to protect ourselves from forces bent on attacking us. It's a new day. How we got here may be worthy of debate, particularly if it exposes the foolish U.S. policies that destroyed anti-Islamist forces in the Middle East and thus brought us to this unfortunate pass. But that can't save us from the threat we now face.

*"The panic in Washington and other
Western capitals is misplaced."*

The United States Should Not Intervene in Iraq

Ivan Eland

*Ivan Eland is a senior fellow and director of the Center on Peace
and Liberty. In the following viewpoint, he argues that the Islamic State of Iraq and Syria (ISIS) is focused on sectarian
battles in the region and is no real threat to the United States.
Eland says that past US interventions in Iraq have created more
strife and radicalization rather than less. He concludes that there
is no strategic reason for the United States to intervene in Iraq
or against ISIS.*

As you read, consider the following questions:

1. What does Eland say led to the creation of al Qaeda in
   Iraq?

2. What solution for Iraq did Eland advocate in his book
   Partitioning for Peace?

3. How should the United States secure oil supplies, according to Eland?

Despite all of the hysteria surrounding the advances in northern Iraq of the brutal group Islamic State of Iraq and Syria (ISIS), no crisis exists for U.S. security, and the American people are wise in their skepticism of renewed U.S. military involvement in that country. Even if the gains of the group eventually lead to an even bigger regional conflagration, in which most of the boundaries of the artificial states in the region originally set by the colonial powers are washed away, good riddance. Those boundaries, which divide ethnic and sectarian areas, have led to much conflict in the past and to the rise of leaders using autocratic methods—such as Bashar al-Assad in Syria and Saddam Hussein and Nouri al-Maliki in Iraq—as the only means to dampen the conflict among restive groups. As U.S. news commentators tell us that the Syrian civil war—where ethno-sectarian groups similar to those in Iraq, the Shi'ites (in Syria, they are called the Alawites), Sunnis, and Kurds, are fighting—has been exported to Iraq, they don't go back in history far enough. The commentators imply that the [Barack] Obama administration should have provided more military aid to the moderate Syrian opposition, thus somehow checking the growth of the ISIS and its migration back to Iraq. Yes migration back to Iraq, where it originated as al Qaeda in Iraq in opposition to George W. Bush's ill-advised U.S. invasion of Iraq in 2003.

The United States Facilitated the Rise of ISIS

Americans have a short historical memory, usually to their government's benefit. For example, people still crow about smashing [Adolf] Hitler's Third Reich in World War II, forgetting that U.S. government actions helped bring Hitler to power in the first place—for example, the unnecessary U.S. intervention to help France and Britain win World War I, then looking the other way while these powers humiliated the Germans politically and economically, and finally Woodrow Wilson's demand that Kaiser Wilhelm II abdicate, thus paving the way for Hitler's rise. Similarly, the U.S. government encouraged and funded Islamist radicalism during the Cold War to combat the Soviet Union in insignificant hellholes in the developing world. Doing so led to the creation of al Qaeda and the 9/11 attacks [referring to the September 11, 2001, terrorist attacks on the United States].

A longer memory in this situation leads us back to the foolish U.S. invasion of Iraq, which created al Qaeda in Iraq in opposition. The group then migrated to the civil war in neighboring Syria, where it took strategic assets, such as weapons caches and oil facilities, while astutely avoiding fighting the superior forces of the Syrian government. There, the group also changed its name to the Islamic State of Iraq and Syria (ISIS). It then moved back into Iraq, and its 800–1,200 fighters are marching toward the northern outskirts of Baghdad, a city of more than seven million people. ISIS has much combat experience and has captured heavy weapons given by the United States to the now fleeing Iraqi army. Yet ISIS seems sophisticated in avoiding fights when it can by seemingly buying off Iraqi army commanders to get them to order their troops to scram rather than offer resistance. The group's fighters learned this tactic firsthand from the U.S. occupation of Iraq, when American general David Petraeus essentially bribed moderate Sunni tribal leaders to fight them.

No Crisis

Yet the panic in Washington and other Western capitals is misplaced. It's time for Obama, who has such innate tendencies, to again have a [Dwight] Eisenhower moment, conclude that no crisis exists, and minimize U.S. involvement in this burgeoning mess. Remember that during the U.S. occupation, the United States also faced fierce Shi'ite militias, which are now coming to the defense of Baghdad and the Shi'ite Maliki government. Since Baghdad is half Shi'ite and the southern part of Iraq is heavily Shi'ite, the Sunni ISIS insurgency, which feeds off the Shi'ite government's oppression of Sunnis, will not get much traction in those areas.

Thus, the insurgents will probably be stopped in Baghdad and a partition of the country may ensue, as the Kurdish militias in northern Iraq have taken advantage of the chaos to grab the oil-rich city of Kirkuk. The Kurds already have an autonomous region and, with the likely Sunni-Shi'ite bloodletting to come, may wisely try to stay out of it, as they have done in neighboring Syria.

In 2009, I wrote a book called *Partitioning for Peace: An Exit Strategy for Iraq* in which I called for a negotiated partition (soft partition) of Iraq into a confederation of autonomous regions, with a weak central government. The thought was that in an artificial country, such as Iraq, with a history of one ethno-sectarian group commandeering the government and using it to oppress the other groups, a week central government would make all groups feel more secure and lead to greater stability. I also predicted that if Iraq were not partitioned softly, it would . . . face partition by war (a hard partition). Since the book was written, Syria, with the same groups involved, has already been effectively partitioned by ethno-sectarian conflict.

Senator John McCain and other hawks always want more U.S. intervention in Syria, Iraq, and everywhere else. Yet as they were advocating shipping more U.S. weapons to the moderate opposition in Syria, ISIS was picking up heavy U.S. weapons left behind by the fleeing U.S.-supplied Iraqi army. In chaotic civil war situations, the nastiest groups always end up with the arms, no matter whom they are given to initially. McCain has also claimed that the United States had defeated in Iraq what is now ISIS, but that the Obama administration blew that accomplishment by not leaving a residual force in Iraq. In my most recent book, *The Failure of Counterinsurgency: Why Hearts and Minds Are Seldom Won*, the study of many historical guerrilla campaigns led me to [baseball star] Yogi Berra's famous conclusion that it "ain't over till it's over." As in many other examples of guerrilla warfare, the guerrillas are not beaten until the grievance that is their reason for fighting has been addressed. General Petraeus got the best result he could for the U.S. in Iraq—dampening the insurgency temporarily with bribery until the United States could extract itself—but the insurgency will never be extinguished until the Shi'ite oppression of Sunnis is halted. However, calls in the United States for Maliki to be "more inclusive" in his government smack of culturally insensitive and naïve political correctness. In an Iraq with no history or culture of multi-ethno-sectarian democracy, partition is probably the only pragmatic route to stability and prosperity, unless of course a ruthless dictator, such as Saddam, is brought back.

No War for Oil

Also, anyone watching American news shows is led to believe that what happens in Iraq and the Middle East region is vital to U.S. security because much oil is produced there. In my 2011 book, *No War for Oil: U.S. Dependency and the Middle East*, I debunk the myth among governments that oil is any more strategic than any other commodity or product. Thus it is cheaper to just buy the oil rather than create expensive military forces to fight for it and prevent a cutoff of supplies that will probably never occur.

Finally, won't ISIS use any territory acquired as a base to launch terrorist attacks on the United States? This outcome will probably happen only if the United States actively aids the Iraqi government by providing it with more military equipment (risky, given what happened to the last equipment given) or directly attacking ISIS with air strikes. Yet the group seems to be so preoccupied with setting up a Sunni state in the Middle East that it has been reluctant to fight even the Syrian government. So further U.S. intervention will probably just increase instability by making the Shi'ite Iraqi government unwilling to accept a more stable partition of the region and lead to blowback terrorist attacks on the United States. Therefore, the United States should resist getting involved again in the Iraqi quagmire.

> *"A successful intervention would require far more massive and comprehensive measures, and in the absence of these, limited steps might be the worst of all worlds."*

Limited Airstrikes Against ISIS a Bad Idea

Daniel L. Byman

Daniel L. Byman is the research director of the Center for Middle East Policy at the Brookings Institution. In the following viewpoint, he argues that air strikes will do little good against the Islamic State of Iraq and Syria (ISIS). Instead, he says that the United States needs a broader strategy for the region. He argues that then Iraqi prime minister Nouri al-Maliki alienated other countries in the region, as well as parts of Iraq's population, and that this hampered the fight against ISIS. Byman concludes that without confronting the underlying problems, air strikes may just make things worse in the region.

As you read, consider the following questions:

1. Byman says the size and strength of the Iraqi army are not the problem, but what does he say is?

2. Which of America's allies in the region does Byman believe would oppose US action on behalf of Maliki?

3. What role does Byman believe the Kurds could play in the battle against ISIS?

The Islamic State of Iraq and al-Sham (ISIS) is metastasizing, with its forces spreading across Iraq and threatening Baghdad. Much of the world is aghast as this brutal insurgent and terrorist group seems to grow in power, and much of the world is groping for ways to intervene effectively. Iraq's hard-pressed regime has called on the United States to provide air power to help it defeat ISIS, and U.S. administration officials are weighing limited airstrikes. However, such a move would represent the triumph of tactics over strategy. A successful intervention would require far more massive and comprehensive measures, and in the absence of these, limited steps might be the worst of all worlds.

From afar, surgical strikes seem like an ideal way to intervene. They appear decisive, yet because they do not involve American boots on the ground, they limit risk. If the United States were to deploy fixed-wing aircrafts or drones, so the thinking goes, it could destroy some of ISIS's forces. This would make it harder for ISIS to mass its troops and move quickly from one area to the next, as large formations and moving targets are particularly vulnerable to U.S. air power. Bombing might offer a morale boost for the beleaguered Iraqi forces, showing them that the United States and its powerful military are on their side. And back in Washington, a limited campaign would answer demands to "do something" about a deteriorating military situation in a country where America lost over 4,000 soldiers and spent billions of dollars, offering an opportunity for the president to look strong.

Yet limited bombing has many downsides. Currently, the United States lacks the intelligence on Iraq and ISIS necessary to carry out anything more than opportunistic strikes. The

United States has begun the process of gaining this intelligence, but getting a comprehensive picture will take months, if not longer. ISIS is an irregular army that does not rely on tanks or other mechanized forces to achieve victory, making it hard for air power to deal a decisive blow. Although its convoys flying black flags would be easy targets, it would quickly adapt—becoming more discreet and traveling in smaller units if U.S. aircraft threatened to attack.

In any event, the size and strength of the Iraqi army are not the problem—it outmans and outguns ISIS by orders of magnitude. Rather, the Iraqi army's problems involve leadership and morale. Prime Minister Nouri al-Maliki has systematically isolated Iraq's Sunni and Kurdish communities and politicized the officer corps. Unsurprisingly, many Iraqis don't want to fight for what they see as Maliki's personal militia. Maliki has dismissed several officers due to the army's recent dismal performance, but the perception that the army is Shiite-dominated remains and perhaps has even grown as many Sunnis and Kurds deserted during the ISIS advances of the last week.

If the Iraqi army withers and runs when attacked, limited airstrikes will ultimately do little to push ISIS back. Air power can't conquer territory by itself. Even in the best circumstances, airstrikes must be sustained to have a strategic effect. And strikes must work in tandem with advances on the ground, so Iraqi forces can move in and occupy any territory from which ISIS withdraws. If strikes are limited in duration, ISIS can simply lie low, camouflaging its forces among the civilian population and avoiding the offensive until the spotlight moves off Iraq, as it inevitably will. If its forces are hit in one area, it can simply reoccupy the territory when the bombing ends. The United States must be prepared to strike often and repeatedly if it is going to play a major role in pushing ISIS back. This could take months even if all goes well.

The NATO effort to overthrow Libyan dictator Muammar al-Qaddafi in 2011 teaches us many lessons. The good news is that in Libya the opposition was able to stabilize the front with the help of NATO air power. However, pushing back Qaddafi's forces required European special operations forces and the opposition to provide the necessary intelligence to call in airstrikes. Opposition forces then moved in on the ground to take the territory Qaddafi's forces abandoned. Their morale was high as they believed they were fighting for a free Libya. Most importantly from a military point of view, the campaign took several months and involved over 25,000 sorties—a far more massive effort than what is being considered in Iraq.

Making the problem even more complex is the interplay between Iraq and Syria, and the region as a whole. Al Qaeda in Iraq, which renamed itself ISIS (and, to add confusion, has since been rejected by the al Qaeda core), began in Iraq but moved the core of its operations to Syria. This was both part of a genuine desire to topple Syrian president Bashar al-Assad and because the group was hard-pressed in Iraq. As it regrouped and grew in Syria, it expanded operations in Iraq, culminating in the recent offensive. Pushing ISIS back in Iraq is beneficial, but as long as it retains a base in Syria this is only a short-term solution. Even worse is that the problem is spreading throughout the region. Two and a half million refugees from Syria have fled the conflict. This flow, along with the passions generated by the slaughter of the Syrian (and now Iraqi) civil wars, has increased unrest in Jordan and has inflamed sectarian passions in Lebanon, where violence has grown and threatens to increase further.

If the United States bombs Iraq now, it will once again become tarred with the brush of Iraq—whether Washington likes it or not. At a time when sectarian fervor is at a fever pitch, the United States will be seen as taking sides, in this case on behalf of a pro-Iranian regime. America's allies in the region such as Saudi Arabia and the United Arab Emirates are vehemently anti-Iran and scorn Maliki as Tehran's puppet. They are already suspicious that U.S. talks with Iran are cover for a broader alliance with Tehran and would resent an intervention on behalf of Maliki, as would many Sunnis. These allies may become even more critical of a nuclear deal and broader rapprochement with Iran and conclude that the United States is secretly working to keep Iran's other ally, the Assad regime, in power.

Putting regional rivalries aside, the Maliki regime is part of the problem. The Shiite prime minister has used corruption, brutality, religious discrimination, and the politicization of the security services to strengthen his grip on power. By militarily supporting the regime, the United States will be associated with Maliki's rule, no matter how many reforms the country demands as quid pro quo.

A few surgical strikes to hit ISIS forces and leaders is not enough. A truly successful intervention would require far more time and effort on the part of the United States. The good news is that there may be more time than the ominous headlines of Baghdad's imminent fall suggest. ISIS has so far advanced primarily through Sunni Arab areas, and it will face a much tougher fight as it approaches Baghdad and the Shiite heartland. A one-off set of strikes, particularly if they were divorced from a ground campaign, would offer at best limited military advantages, but would be more likely to produce little lasting effect and might even backfire. The use of force, even limited force, must be linked to a broader strategy for Iraq and for the region as a whole.

The first step is to stop ISIS from spreading further. The spread of violence in Iraq was utterly predictable, and there is no reason to think it will stop there. The United States should help shore up the regimes in Lebanon and Jordan, providing financial support to manage surging Syrian and Iraqi refugee populations and providing assistance to those regimes' security forces to police their borders. This aid will not stop ISIS in Iraq or Syria, but it can help prevent ISIS, and regional instability in general, from spreading further.

The Obama administration should also encourage the Maliki regime and the Kurds to work closely together. Both oppose ISIS, and as Iraq expert Michael Knights points out, the Kurds sit astride ISIS's lines of advance in Iraq and their military forces are capable and coherent. If they join the fray, they can deal severe blows to ISIS. Bringing the Kurds into the fray would help push ISIS back, and to make a deal, Maliki would have to broaden his government to reflect Kurdish desires for more autonomy—a good thing for Iraq as a whole though a step Maliki will hesitate to take.

At the same time, Washington should continue to step up intelligence gathering. In both Iraq and Syria, the United States needs precise information on ISIS's forces and its leaders—information that would make any military campaign far more effective. The United States undertook such an effort before in Iraq led by Gen. Stanley McChrystal and the Joint Special Operations Command, but this took time and resources, with hundreds of intelligence personnel and operators involved. Even more valuable now would be resuming the work the United States left unfinished when its forces departed Iraq at the end of 2011: large-scale training of the Iraqi military and pushing for the associated political reforms. The United States attempted a massive training program while its hundreds of thousands of troops were in Iraq—an effort that saw notable success. But this success has been undermined by Maliki's politicization of the officer corps since the U.S. departure. Successful training will thus be more than a technical problem; it will require the Iraqi regime to take the political steps necessary to build a professional military. This will be a tall order for Maliki.

Finally, the United States must harmonize its Iraq and Syria policies and develop an overall regional strategy. As the 2011 unrest in Syria has turned to violence and then to civil war, U.S. policy in the region has been reactive. The United States needs to more aggressively back moderate Syrian opposition forces, many of which are strongly opposed to ISIS. It may be too late to topple Assad (especially in the near term), but when combined with a more effective Iraqi military, these forces can put pressure on ISIS on both sides of the border.

To stop ISIS and make the region more stable, the Obama administration needs to ensure that any use of force is embedded in a broader strategy. Otherwise, all that limited bombing offers is the illusion that America is acting decisively, and it could make a bad situation worse.

Periodical and Internet Sources Bibliography

The following articles have been selected to supplement the diverse views presented in this chapter.

Max Boot	"How ISIS Can Be Defeated," *Newsweek*, February 17, 2015.
Noam Chomsky	"To Deal with ISIS, U.S. Should Own Up to Chaos of Iraq War and Other Radicalizing Acts," *Democracy Now!*, March 3, 2015.
Josh Cohen	"With 580 U.S. Boots on the Ground in Ukraine, What's Vladimir Putin's Next Move?," *Reuters*, April 23, 2015.
Stephen Collinson	"What Will Putin Do if U.S. Arms Ukraine?," *CNN*, February 6, 2015.
Francis Fukuyama	"Dealing with ISIS," *American Interest*, March 23, 2015.
FoxNews.com	"US Troops in Europe Request Bigger Guns amid Tensions with Russia over Ukraine," April 26, 2015.
Daniel R. Green	"Our Own Worst Enemy: How America Defeated Itself in Afghanistan," *Foreign Policy*, April 7, 2015.
Jeff Schogol	"U.S. Readies Afghans to Fly Solo," *Air Force Times*, April 27, 2015.
Michael D. Shear and Mark Mazzetti	"U.S. to Delay Pullout of Troops from Afghanistan to Aid Strikes," *New York Times*, March 25, 2015.
Lizzy Tomei	"It's 2015. Time for Some New U.S. Operations in Iraq and Afghanistan," *The Week*, January 22, 2015.

CHAPTER 3

What Are US Military Personnel Issues?

Chapter Preface

The US military has a serious problem with sexual assault, according to United States senator Kirsten Gillibrand, D-NY. Gillibrand, in her role as a member of the Personnel Subcommittee of the Senate Committee on Armed Services, has been working on sexual assault cases in the military for years. In May 2015, she said that the problem with military sexual assaults was worse than generally reported in Department of Defense (DOD) surveys because those surveys did not include civilian victims in its data. The senator did get the DOD to release information about 107 sexual assault cases, more than half of which involved civilian victims. She "found punishments that were too lenient and the word of the alleged assailant was more likely to be believed than the victim. Less than a quarter of the cases went to trial and just 11 resulted in conviction for a sex crime," according to an Associated Press report in a May 2015 article at the Business Insider website.

Some commentators have called the sexual assault problem in the military an "epidemic." The *Week*, for example, pointed out in a March 2013 article that "female soldiers today are 180 times more likely to be sexually assaulted by a fellow soldier than killed by an enemy." A 2012 anonymous survey of eleven hundred women who served in Afghanistan and Iraq reported that nearly half said they had been sexually harassed, and almost a quarter said they had been assaulted. Yet, a 2011 study found that out of nineteen thousand or more incidents, only three thousand were reported. Reporting can be difficult in the military's hierarchical chain of command, where those with higher rank can be difficult to hold to account. Virginia Messick, who was one of sixty-two trainees assaulted by instructors at Lackland Air Force Base between 2009 and 2012, asked in the *Week* article, "How am I supposed to go about reporting something when the person I'm supposed to report to is the person who raped me?"

On the other hand, Rosa Brooks, a law professor at Georgetown University, dislikes the use of the term "epidemic" when referring to sexual assaults in the military. She argues in a 2013 article in *Foreign Policy* that calling the military's sexual assault problem a crisis "conceals the progress the military has made in developing effective sexual assault prevention and response programs, and it distracts us from the even higher rates of sexual violence in comparable civilian populations." She argues that rates of sexual assault in the military "appear to be substantially lower than rates of sexual assault in comparable civilian populations," and that the military has a higher reporting rate than the rest of society.

Other military personnel issues, including the treatment of gay and lesbian service members, women in combat roles, and the reinstatement of the draft, are explored in the chapter that follows.

"Since the draft ended four decades ago, the public has been removed from decisions on military intervention and our presidents more adventuresome."

The United States Should Reinstate the Draft

Thom Serafin

Thom Serafin is the founder and chief executive officer of the Chicago-based communications firm Serafin & Associates. In the following viewpoint, he argues that the abolition of the draft means that most Americans are not affected when the United States goes to war. As a result, he says, politicians can commit troops to endless conflicts without any resistance from the American people. Reinstituting a draft would force the United States to confront the cost of its wars directly and would result in a much more restrained foreign policy.

As you read, consider the following questions:

1. How does Serafin say the invasion of Iraq was financed?

2. Why does Serafin feel that talk about "war weariness" is misleading?

Thom Serafin, "Bring Back the Draft to Make Clear the Cost of War," *Chicago Sun Times*, January 9, 2014. Copyright © 2014 CHICAGO SUN-TIMES. All rights reserved. Reproduced with permission.

3. In addition to the draft, what else does Serafin say the United States should reinstate?

The cruel execution of American journalist James Foley by Islamic fanatics [in Syria] has reopened the debate about how and when the United States should decide on military intervention. It would be a shame, however, if our political leaders let themselves be guided by public opinion polls that react to events rather than full debates that weigh the risks against the possible benefits of going to war. That is a debate that needs to take place now, given that the White House and the Pentagon are not on the same page and President [Barack] Obama acknowledges we "don't have a strategy yet."

The End of the Draft

When the draft was ended in 1973, it became all too easy for American presidents to intervene militarily anywhere without the kind of public scrutiny and opposition that developed after the Vietnam War destroyed thousands of young lives in an endless, unwinnable conflict.

By contrast, in World War II, volunteers and draftees fought together with the backing of a public that sacrificed comforts and endured rationing to support the war effort. To maintain that support, Franklin Delano Roosevelt outlined goals that justified the enormous cost in lives and money.

Since the draft ended four decades ago, the public has been removed from decisions on military intervention and our presidents more adventuresome. The invasion and occupation of Iraq [in 2003] was not financed by a tax increase. It was fought on the nation's credit card and it helped wipe out a projected $5.6 trillion budget surplus to create a huge deficit by 2008.

In an eloquent, prescient speech in 2002, the late Senator Robert Byrd warned that Iraq would be a turning point: "The idea that the United States or any other nation can legitimately attack a nation that is not imminently threatening, but may be threatening in the future—is a radical new twist on the traditional idea of self-defense. It appears to be in contravention of international law and the UN [United Nations] charter." Yet, he added, "There is no debate, no discussion, no attempt to lay out for the nation the pros and cons of this particular war."

Current talk about "war weariness" by pundits is a little misleading, because the sacrifice in Iraq and Afghanistan has been borne by a small segment of the population who did the fighting, lost their lives, limbs and in many cases suffered grievously from PTSD [post-traumatic stress disorder]. These men and women return to communities largely insulated from the domestic sacrifice of previous wars and understand little about the horrors these veterans have endured in multiple deployments.

The Long War

With more than 700 military installations across the world and a defense budget nearly equal to the combined budgets of all other nations, there is a reflex by successive U.S. administrations to use that military strength to solve diplomatic challenges. Instead of war as a last resort, military planners like former CIA [Central Intelligence Agency] director General [David] Petraeus write about readiness for "the long war" lasting a hundred years.

Critics of this doctrine, such as military historian Col. Andrew Bacevich, argue that in the long wars in Iraq and Afghanistan, "Washington committed that military to an endeavor that it manifestly cannot win."

Writing in 2010 he observed: "The truth is we're lost in the desert, careening down an unmarked road, odometer busted, GPS on the fritz, and fuel gauge hovering just above E. Washington can only hope that the American people, napping in the backseat, won't notice."

The Quality of Draftees

But what got [Secretary of Defense Donald] Rumsfeld in a world of trouble was his casual insult of millions of veterans who have been drafted into this nation's military service over the last half century and served their country with honor. Veterans' organizations were devastated by Rumsfeld's comment that the service of draftees added "no value, no advantage, really" to the military. Particularly in the case of young men who had been killed or wounded, it seemed coldly insensitive to use phrases like "sucked into the intake" to describe their military service. It was unclear why Rumsfeld assumed that most draftees did not serve in good faith, despite our historical experience to the contrary. A 2002 report ... noted that, in a draft era, draftees actually have lower rates of desertion than soldiers who volunteer, and the reason was that draftees tended on average to be of higher quality. A book praised as a "definitive account of the draft" reported that draftees during the Vietnam [War] era were better behaved and superior in education, intelligence, and maturity in comparison to volunteers. The Vietnam draft didn't lower the quality of the military; it actually kept it from getting worse. Something else must have been going on for Rumsfeld to be so dismissive of young men who have answered their country's call and served to the best of their abilities.

Diane H. Mazur, A More Perfect Military:
How the Constitution Can Make Our Military Stronger.
New York: Oxford University Press, 2010, p. 129.

Unfortunately, the consent of the governed—the American people—has been the missing element in these debates on when we go to war. Political leaders would rather rely on public opinion polls than explain to American citizens why they are willing to commit American forces to a military conflict. That would change if a military draft was reinstated. Last year, a bill was introduced in the House of Representatives that would require 30 million people, men and women, between the ages of 18 and 25 to perform two years of national service in either the armed services or in civilian life. It would build upon the community service infrastructure already in place such as the Peace Corps and AmeriCorps, as well as local initiatives such as NYC Serve.

It is time to reinstate the draft and a war tax, which would give the American people a genuine stake in decisions on foreign policy that can no longer be entrusted solely to the elites in Washington.

> "Rescinding the policy that has excluded women since 1994 from serving in direct ground combat positions will strengthen the military."

Women Should Be Allowed in Combat Roles

Cheryl Pellerin

Cheryl Pellerin is a science writer and reporter. In the following viewpoint, she reports that the Department of Defense (DOD) is moving to open up many positions to women that were previously reserved for men. The defense secretary at the time the viewpoint was written, Leon Panetta, says this will strengthen the armed forces. Panetta also points out in the viewpoint that women often already effectively serve in combat roles. Pellerin says an evaluation of all jobs in the armed forces should be completed by 2016.

As you read, consider the following questions:

1. According to Pellerin, what will happen if one of the services decides to close a position to women?

2. According to the viewpoint, how much of the armed forces is made up of women, and how many women have deployed to Iraq and Afghanistan?

Cheryl Pellerin, "Dempsey: Allowing Women in Combat Strengthens Joint Force," American Forces Press Service, January 24, 2013. Courtesy of US Department of Defense.

3. What does US Army general Martin E. Dempsey say was the moment he decided more military jobs needed to be open to women?

Rescinding the policy that has excluded women since 1994 from serving in direct ground combat positions will strengthen the military, the chairman of the Joint Chiefs of Staff said here today [in January 2013].

Opening Positions to Women

Army Gen. Martin E. Dempsey joined Defense Secretary Leon E. Panetta at a Pentagon news conference to announce the decision and to sign a joint memorandum that sets the process in motion.

"Today we are acting to expand the opportunities for women to serve in the United States armed forces and to better align our policies with the experiences we have had over the past decade of war," Dempsey said. "Ultimately, we're acting to strengthen the joint force."

As part of the new policy, the services are reviewing about 53,000 positions now closed by unit but that will be open to women who meet standards developed for the positions.

According to senior defense officials, the services are also reviewing about 184,000 positions now closed by specialty but that will be open to women who meet the standards.

Gender-neutral occupational standards are specific requirements for anyone who wants to qualify for a specific job, an official explained. This is different from a physical fitness test, which is a general assessment of fitness that is normed for gender and age throughout the services.

If any of the services recommend that a specific position be closed to women, the secretary of defense must personally approve that recommendation, the official said. Panetta directed the military departments to submit detailed implementation plans by May 15 and to move ahead to integrate women into previously closed positions. The secretary directed the process to be complete by Jan. 1, 2016.

Women make up about 15 percent, or nearly 202,400, of the U.S. military's 1.4 million active-duty personnel. Over the past decade, more than 280,000 women have deployed in support of operations in Iraq and Afghanistan, and 152 of them have died.

Women Already in Combat

Many women in uniform, Dempsey said, already have served in combat, recalling his arrival in Baghdad as commander of the 1st Armored Division in 2003. During his first foray out of the forward operating base, he said, he hopped into an up-armored Humvee [high mobility multipurpose wheeled vehicle (HMMWV)].

"I asked the driver who he was [and] where he was from," Dempsey recalled, "then I slapped the turret gunner around the leg and said, 'Who are you?' She leaned down and said, 'I'm Amanda.'"

The female turret-gunner was protecting her division commander, the chairman said, "and it's from that point on that I realized something had changed and it was time to do something about it."

The Joint Chiefs share common cause on the need to start the process of integrating women into combat-related jobs that have been closed to them, and to do it right, Dempsey said.

"We're committed to a purposeful and a principled approach," he said, adding that the Joint Chiefs developed a set of guiding principles for successfully integrating women into previously restricted occupational fields.

The department and the services will extend opportunities to women in a way that maintains readiness, morale and unit cohesion and preserves warfighting capability, Dempsey said, to uphold the nation's trust and confidence.

© Daryl Cagle, CagleCartoons.com.

"We'll also integrate women in a way that enhances opportunity for everyone. This means setting clear standards of performance for all occupations based on what it actually takes to do the job," the chairman explained.

"It also means ensuring that these standards are gender-neutral in occupations that will open to women," he added.

137

The services and U.S. Special Operations Command will begin expanding the number of units and the number of women assigned to those units this year, the chairman said.

"They will continue to assess, develop and validate gender-neutral standards so we can start assigning personnel to previously closed occupations," he added. "And they will take the time needed to do the work without compromising the principles I just mentioned."

Adherence to the principles may lead to an assessment that some specialties and ratings should remain exceptions, he noted.

"In some cases, however, the services will bear the responsibility for providing the thorough analysis needed to better understand and better articulate what's best for the Joint Force and the women who serve in it," the chairman said.

Women will continue to serve with distinction throughout the armed forces, he said, in and out of combat, on land and at sea and in the air.

"We all wear the same uniform and we all fire the same weapons," he added. "And most importantly, we all take the same oath."

"Even in the non-contact sports of golf, tennis, and volleyball, men compete with men, women against women."

Do We Need Women in Combat?

Patrick J. Buchanan

Patrick J. Buchanan is a political commentator and the author of Suicide of a Superpower: Will America Survive to 2025? *In the following viewpoint, he argues that women's serving in combat roles is contrary to history, nature, and military necessity. Buchanan says that women have never fought in wars before and that they do not compete with men in sports. He argues that women were not needed to fight previous wars. He blames the movement of women into combat roles on a radical feminist agenda, and he feels it is a betrayal of the ideals of the United States.*

As you read, consider the following questions:

1. According to Buchanan, who did the Third Reich send into war rather than women?

2. What does Buchanan say are the closest approximations to war in civilian life?

Patrick J. Buchanan, "Do We Need Women in Combat?," *The American Conservative*, June 25, 2013. Copyright © 2013 AMERICAN CONSERVATIVE. All rights reserved. Reproduced with permission.

3. Buchanan suggests that what crime among soldiers may have been encouraged by women in the military?

"The Pentagon unveiled plans Tuesday for fully integrating women into front-line and special combat roles, including elite forces such as Army Rangers and Navy SEALs."

So ran the lead on the CNN story. And why are we doing this? Did the young officers leading troops in battle in Afghanistan and Iraq, returning with casualties, say they needed women to enhance the fighting efficiency of their combat units and the survival rate of their soldiers?

Did men from the 101st and 82nd Airborne, the Marines, the SEALs and Delta Force petition the Joint Chiefs to put women alongside them in future engagements to make them an even superior force?

No. This decision to put women in combat represents a capitulation of the military brass, a surrender to the spirit of our age, the Pentagon's salute to feminist ideology.

This is not a decision at which soldiers arrived when they studied after-action reports but the product of an ideology that contradicts human nature, human experience and human history, and declares as dogma that women are just as good at soldiering as men. But if this were true, rather than merely asserted, would it have taken mankind the thousands of years from Thermopylae to discover it?

In the history of civilization, men have fought the wars. In civilized societies, attacks on women have always been regarded as contemptible and cowardly. Even the Third Reich in its dying hours did not send women into battle, but old men and boys. "You don't hit a girl!" was something every American boy had drilled into him from childhood. It was part of our culture, the way we were raised. A Marine friend told me he would have resigned from the Corps rather than fight women with the pugil sticks used for bayonet practice at Parris Island.

Sending women into combat on equal terms seems also to violate common sense. When they reach maturity, men are bigger, stronger, more aggressive. Thus they commit many times the number of violent crimes and outnumber women in prisons 10 to 1. For every Bonnie Parker, there are 10 Clyde Barrows.

Is it a coincidence that every massacre discussed in our gun debate—from the Texas Tower to the Long Island Railroad, from Columbine to Fort Hood, from Virginia Tech to Tucson, from Aurora to Newtown—was the work of a crazed male?

Nothing matches mortal combat where soldiers fight and kill, and are wounded, maimed and die for cause or country. Domestically, the closest approximations are combat training, ultimate fighting, boxing and that most physical of team sports, the NFL.

Yet no women compete against men in individual or team sports. They are absent from boys' and men's teams in high school and college, be it football, basketball, baseball, hockey or lacrosse.

Even in the non-contact sports of golf, tennis, and volleyball, men compete with men, women against women. In the Olympics, to which nations send their best athletes, women and men compete separately in track and field, swimming, and gymnastics.

Consider our own history. Would any U.S. admiral say that in any of America's great naval battles—Mobile Bay, Manila Bay, Midway, the Coral Sea—we would have done better with some women manning the guns?

In the Revolutionary and Civil Wars, World Wars I and II, Korea and Vietnam, women were not in combat. Was it invidious discrimination of which we should all be ashamed that women were not fighting alongside the men at Gettysburg, in the Argonne, at Normandy or with "Chesty" Puller's Marines in the retreat from the Chosin Reservoir?

Undeniably, some women might handle combat as well as some men. But that is true of some 13-, 14- and 15-year-old boys, and some 50- and 60-year-old men. Yet we do not draft boys or men that age or send them into combat. Is this invidious discrimination based on age, or ageism?

Carry this feminist-egalitarian ideology to its logical conclusion and half of those storming the Omaha and Utah beaches should have been girls and women. Is this not an absurdity?

We have had Navy ships become "love boats," with female sailors returning pregnant. At the Naval Academy, three midshipmen, football players, allegedly raped an intoxicated classmate. For months, she was too ashamed and frightened to report it.

An estimated 26,000 personnel of the armed forces were sexually assaulted in 2011, up from 19,000 in 2010. Obama and the Congress are understandably outraged. Such assaults are appalling. But is not the practice of forcing young men and women together in close quarters a contributory factor here?

Among the primary reasons the Equal Rights Amendment, the ERA, went down to defeat three decades ago was the realization it could mean, in a future war, women could be drafted equally with men, and sent in equal numbers into combat.

But what appalled the Reaganites is social progress in the age of Obama. This is another country from the one we grew up in.

*"For me personally it comes down to in-
tegrity—theirs as individuals, and ours
as an institution."*

Don't Ask, Don't Tell Repeal Has Been a Success for the Military and for Gay Rights

Lisa Daniel

*Lisa Daniel is a writer for American Forces Press Service. In the
following viewpoint, she reports on the repeal of Don't Ask,
Don't Tell. The policy stated that gay and lesbian individuals
serving in the US military had to conceal their sexual orientation or be discharged from the service. The law was repealed in
2011. Despite arguments that the repeal would cause serious
problems, it caused no stir for most in the military. However,
Daniel reports, gay and lesbian individuals in the military were
largely relieved and reported being able to do their jobs better
now that they did not have to hide their sexual orientation.*

As you read, consider the following questions:

1. According to Daniel, senior military leaders say that the
   repeal of Don't Ask, Don't Tell has had what impact on
   military readiness?

Lisa Daniel, "Nine Months After Repeal, Gay Troops Slowly Come Out," American
Forces Press Service, June 20, 2012. Courtesy of US Department of Defense.

2. According to the viewpoint, who is Mike Mullen, and what role did he have in the repeal of Don't Ask, Don't Tell?

3. How many service members were discharged under Don't Ask, Don't Tell?

In the nine months since being given the legal right to serve openly in the military, gay service members are increasingly speaking out about the double lives they led under the "Don't Ask, Don't Tell" law.

Life in the Closet

As gay, lesbian, bisexual and transgender Americans and their supporters celebrate June as "Pride Month," two senior officers—a navy woman and an army man, both with more than 20 years of service—accepted a request to speak about the issue to foreign journalists visiting the Pentagon.

The officers asked not to be named because of the personal nature of the information they shared. They told of the stress of serving two decades on a job in which they lived in guarded secrecy about their personal lives and constant worry of being exposed—and discharged—under the law.

"It was the secrets, the trying to guard every word so that you don't use the wrong pronoun," the soldier said, recalling his fear of referring to his partner as "he."

"That eats at your soul," he added, "and you feel pretty hollow when you have to live that kind of lie."

While senior military leaders say the change has had no impact on readiness and little to no effect on most of the 1.2 million members on active duty, gay troops describe the repeal's effect on them as life-changing.

During three war deployments, the soldier said, he could not bond with others as they decompressed from the fighting to learn about each other—their families, influences, and world views. "It wreaks havoc on your ability to deal with stress," he said.

Back home, even calls he'd receive from his leaders on weekends were stressful, the soldier said. "Every time my phone rang and I saw the caller ID," he recalled, "I thought, 'I'm about to be fired. Every single time I got called at home, regardless of the reason for the call, for a split second, I thought, 'This will be the call where I get fired.' It was always in the back of my head."

When the law's repeal took effect Sept. 20 [2011] "with a collective yawn" from the straight military community, he said, "there was this feeling of relief [among gay troops] that not only do I now finally feel like a full-fledged citizen of this country—the country that I put my life on the line to defend more than once—but now I can do my job more efficiently."

While the military as a whole goes through its transformation with openness, individual members contemplate how far to go with theirs. Other than being named in the media, the soldier now lives an openly gay life. He recently married his partner of 12 years here. The couple hopes to adopt a child—a prospect that was impossible before, the soldier said, because "the idea of teaching a child to lie in order to protect his fathers was an ethical nonstarter."

[One] sailor has continued to stay quiet about her personal life, but says the repeal has given her the freedom and confidence not to lie about who she is.

"If you ask, I will tell you," she said. "That's the decision I made on Sept. 20. While I'm not going to stand up and announce it, I also won't turn a blind eye to those younger members who are putting their lives on the line."

The sailor had to do just that as a lieutenant, she said, when a young enlisted sailor came to her and wanted to confide in her about her own sexuality. "I cut her off and said, 'You cannot say that next sentence that I think you're going to say, because I'm an officer.'" Under Don't Ask, Don't Tell, the officer would have been required to report it up the chain of command.

It was about the same time that the officer experienced a bitter breakup in a relationship that caused her to put her personal life mostly on hold and reinforced her two decades of silence about who she is. The breakup, with a woman who was leaving the military, became messy. The two owned property together. There were threats of outing the young lieutenant who had hoped to make a career of the military, as so many in her family had.

"I got threatened with being outed," she said. "Being thrown out of the military at the five- or six-year mark wasn't in my plans. . . . It caused me to shut down my life, and I said, 'I'll just do the military thing,' because I just couldn't take the pressure from being threatened."

After Congress passed the repeal in December 2010, the services had to conduct training and do other things to prepare before Defense Department leaders could certify to the president that repeal would not harm readiness. The sailor attended an all-navy training session.

"I caught myself three or four times," she said, "because I was convinced I was going to cry." She was "fundamentally overwhelmed," she said, by the conversation in the room that let her know homosexuality, by and large, had become a non-issue to today's service members.

"I was just so proud that it really had come to the point where this was no big deal," she said.

Others were beginning to see the "disconnect" that she and other gays and lesbians had lamented for years.

"Many other militaries beat us to the punch on this," she noted. When the United States built a 50-nation coalition in Afghanistan, "we didn't go to NATO [North Atlantic Treaty Organization] and say, 'Only deploy your straight people.'"

Life Under Don't Ask, Don't Tell

But the most crushing moment in my life took place four years ago. It was at NAPS [Naval Academy Preparatory School] that I turned myself in under the DADT [Don't Ask, Don't Tell] policy.

After over two years of harassment and hazing while serving overseas—for nothing more than refusing to "prove" my straightness—it had become overwhelmingly clear to me that no matter how well a closeted gay woman or man performed in uniform, and no matter how far we went to protect the secret of our sexuality, we would never be safe from abuse, shame, and the disgrace of a discharge. So four years ago I made the toughest decision of my life—to end my career on my own terms, on the merit of my service, and out myself before I was outed. Under DADT it was never a matter of whether you would be kicked out but a matter of when.

Joseph Christopher Rocha,
"Repeal Is a Testament to the Core Values of the United States,"
The End of Don't Ask, Don't Tell: The Impact in Studies
and Personal Essays by Service Members and Veterans.
Eds. J. Ford Huffman and Tammy S. Schultz. Quantico, VA:
Marine Corps University Press, 2012, p. 176.

And yet those troops served together—ate, slept, showered, fought and bled together—without regard to sexual orientation, she said.

"If you are genuinely operating as a professional military, sexual orientation shouldn't be part of the discussion," she added.

Both officers noted the recent evolution of gay rights in the United States. The military they entered could not have accepted open homosexuality, they acknowledged.

Integrity

"If you served in this military in the 1970s, you would not recognize it now," the sailor said. "People who say we shouldn't serve openly are out of date, out of touch with today's military. The young service members genuinely don't care."

Repeal of Don't Ask, Don't Tell was debated fervently for more than a year, but took effect officially with little fanfare.

"A small group of us went [to the Pentagon office of a former senior civilian leader who is gay], popped a couple bottles of champagne and said, 'Wow. It really did happen,'" the sailor said. "There were plenty of us who, honestly, never thought this day would come."

Now that it has, she added, "I'm convinced you can walk into every office of this building and find someone who is a little more confident in what they do and a little less worried, just because of what has happened in the past six to eight months."

Retired navy [admiral] Mike Mullen is widely credited with being a powerful force behind the repeal of Don't Ask, Don't Tell. As chairman of the Joint Chiefs of Staff, Mullen removed perceived partisanship from the issue by telling a congressional committee in February 2010 that overturning the ban was the right thing to do, and that it would not irreparably harm readiness.

"No matter how I look at the issue, I cannot escape being troubled by the fact that we have in place a policy which forces young men and women to lie about who they are in order to defend their fellow citizens," Mullen said then. "For me, personally, it comes down to integrity—theirs as individuals, and ours as an institution."

Congress voted to repeal the law in December 2010 and President Barack Obama signed a certification to Congress in July 2011 that military leaders agreed that the services were ready to move forward without Don't Ask, Don't Tell.

"I can't say enough about Admiral Mullen's leadership," the sailor said. "It was the leadership of a nonpartisan military that allowed this to happen."

Some 14,500 service members were discharged between 1993 and 2011 under Don't Ask Don't Tell, according to the Servicemembers Legal Defense Network. Some of them are back serving in uniform, the navy officer said, but the Defense Department does not track the numbers.

The navy officer acknowledged that "some incidents have happened" in the military ranks related to gays serving openly. But, she added, they are not enough to roll back the momentum, or the law, in support of gay service members. "It's too big. . . . It's not going to turn this back," she said.

With the legal change, gay service members say they have never been more proud of the U.S. armed forces.

"I've never been more proud of this organization," the army officer said. "I've never been more fully embraced by our military and by our country."

The sailor, who is planning to retire in the next few years, said she has some decisions to make about her post-military life, noting that different regions of the country have different levels of acceptance toward gay people. She said she worries that where she chooses to live out the rest of her life could, effectively, try to put her back in a closet. But this time, she said, she won't go.

"I don't know what I'll do in retirement," she said. "But I won't be hiding."

> *"Transgender service members are increasingly undergoing procedures to align their bodies more closely with the genders with which they identify."*

For Transgender Service Members, Honesty Can End Career

Ernesto Londoño

Ernesto Londoño covers the Pentagon for the Washington Post. *In the following viewpoint, he reports on Landon Wilson, an individual who was honorably discharged from the US Navy after it was revealed that he was transgender. Born a female but identifying with male, Wilson joined the Navy as a woman and began the transition to male while in the service. When it was revealed that Wilson was transgender, his commanders removed him from his post in Afghanistan, and Wilson was discharged. Londoño says that even though Don't Ask, Don't Tell was repealed in 2011, allowing gay and lesbian individuals to serve openly in the military, the repeal did nothing to prevent transgender service members from being dismissed from the armed forces without question if their sexual identity is revealed.*

As you read, consider the following questions:

1. According to Londoño, what did the American Psychiatric Association change its manual to indicate regarding gender nonconformity?

2. By Landon Wilson's estimate, how much did the Navy spend training him for an intelligence job?

3. According to the viewpoint, what did the repeal of Don't Ask, Don't Tell enable?

It felt like the pinnacle of his career, working the graveyard shift in a windowless plywood facility in Afghanistan, monitoring a Special Operations mission as it unfolded in real time on grainy video feeds.

After spending hundreds of thousands of dollars training Landon Wilson to intercept communications, the U.S. military was capitalizing on its investment in the young sailor, already regarded as a rising star in a critical, highly technical field.

But shortly after 2 A.M. on Dec. 7, when a superior tapped him on the back and summoned him outside, one of the secrets that mattered most to Wilson began to unravel.

"This Navy record says female, but this paper says male," the grim-faced sergeant major noted, displaying two sets of personnel records. "So, what are you?"

After an awkward pause, Wilson, who joined the Navy as a woman but who has long felt like a man, provided the answer that set in motion the end of his military career: "I am male."

More than two years after the repeal of the law that barred gay men and lesbians from serving in the military openly, transgender service members can still be dismissed from the force without question, the result of a decades-old policy that dates back to an era when gender nonconformity was widely seen as a mental illness.

The policy, however, is now coming under scrutiny as service members like Wilson become more visible. Transgender service members are increasingly undergoing procedures to align their bodies more closely with the genders with which they identify. Medical experts, meanwhile, are urging the Defense Department to rescind a policy they view as discriminatory and outdated, noting that some of America's closest allies, including Canada, Britain and Australia, have done so seamlessly.

Although the American Psychiatric Association revised its manual last year to indicate gender nonconformity is "not in itself a mental disorder," the Defense Department relies on guidelines that describe transgender individuals as sexual deviants, and their condition as a "paraphilia." Thousands of transgender men and women are now serving in the military while remaining in the closet, according to studies.

"It is a terrible tragedy our people are facing in our great country for no other reason than the fact that they want to express their gender," said Joycelyn Elders, a former U.S. surgeon general who last year co-chaired a study that recommended the military lift its ban on transgender personnel. "We could find no credible medical reason for why transgender persons should be discharged or not allowed in the service."

Drawn to Military Life

Wilson, 24, was born in Warner Robins, a small city in central Georgia that revolved around the namesake Air Force base. An only child raised by a single mother, he recalls feeling he had been assigned the wrong sex as early as infancy.

"Hey, I'm a boy," he recalls blurting out to his mother as a 4-year-old. "The reaction I got was one that even at that young age made me aware that that was not what you were supposed to feel like. So I suppressed it for as long as I could."

As a teenager, Wilson carried himself as a "masculine female," wearing men's clothes and keeping his hair cropped short. A military career appealed to him for the honor that comes with service. But there was another draw, one that researchers say explains why the percentage of transgender people in the U.S. military is twice as high as it is in the civilian population.

"It comes down to the masculinity of it all," Wilson explained. Men struggling with their temptation to transition to women have told researchers that they see military culture as a barrier to keep them from taking the daunting step. In the reverse scenario, Wilson said, it's an easy environment to fit into. "But I think a lot of people look to the military for a new beginning," he added.

As he enlisted, he was urged to become a cryptologic technician. By Wilson's estimate, the Navy spent at least a half-million dollars getting him the highest-level security clearance in government and training him for an intelligence job that involves intercepting and analyzing communications from foreign governments and extremists.

He developed a reputation as a talented, meticulous, hard-working sailor, said Shayne Allen, a former colleague who was stationed with Wilson at the Navy Information Operations Command in Hawaii.

"Landon was someone who you don't see a lot of in the military these days," Allen said. "He not only checked all the boxes, but went above and beyond."

During his time in Hawaii, Wilson earned several awards and accolades for his work. In a unit of roughly 10,000 sailors, he was recognized as the performer of the quarter in 2012 and the enlisted sailor of the quarter in 2013.

A few months after arriving in Hawaii in May 2012, having read up extensively on the issue and connected online with others who had transitioned, Wilson decided to act. He obtained a formal diagnosis of gender identity disorder from a counselor, a step transgender people often take before undergoing hormone therapy. In November, shortly after coming out to his mother, Wilson began taking hormones once a week—which he described as terrifying and exhilarating.

"I knew everything that was on the table, but at the same time it was completely worth it," he said. "It was like taking my first breath."

The effects were almost immediate for Wilson. The injections deepened his voice and molded his face structure and body shape. His muscles and strength grew, along with light facial hair. Because the therapy triggers a process similar to puberty, it also brought about severe acne.

The onset of his transformation came as gay men and lesbians in the military were starting to reap the benefits of the 2011 repeal of "Don't Ask, Don't Tell," the federal law that barred them from serving openly. The change—which had no bearing on transgender service members—offered a slight relief for Wilson, whom many mistook for a lesbian. But he also felt a degree of resentment.

"I knew that the lesbian and gay community were getting all these freedoms and all their privileges," he said. "There was still that silent T that was completely ignored.

Conflicting Gender Records

Although transgender service members were avid supporters of the repeal, activists who led the effort were careful not to inject the plight of transgender service members into the debate.

"There was a certain reticence to discuss it in any official way with stakeholders for fear of complicating the repeal of Don't Ask, Don't Tell," said Allyson Robinson, a former Army officer and transgender activist. "There was a very clear awareness among all the organizations that worked on Don't Ask, Don't Tell that this issue was going to remain outstanding."

Colleagues noticed Wilson's physical changes, but no one seemed to care. He confided in a few people in the military last year, including Allen.

"I said, no harm no foul there," the 20-year-old said in a phone interview, describing his reaction. "To me you've always been Wilson, whether you're a male or a female."

That distinction became strikingly blurred last summer when Wilson volunteered for a yearlong deployment in Afghanistan. When he arrived at a Navy medical processing center in Virginia, he was assigned to male barracks and given male uniforms on the first day. That afternoon, medical personnel noticed paperwork indicating a female and ordered a pregnancy test, but inexplicably kept him housed and clothed as a man.

"I was like, all right, this is going to get very awkward once they see something," he remembers thinking.

Later that summer, when Wilson arrived to a base in South Carolina for combat training, he again was assigned to male barracks. Wilson's deployment paperwork started reflecting the gender everyone from that point forward assumed him to be. And because his former name, which he has since changed legally, is androgynous, no one asked questions. The men who shared his living quarters assumed he was a man. Wilson said that all the shower facilities he used after basic training included private shower stalls.

The three weeks he spent in there were among the happiest in his life, Wilson said, as he rambled through the woods wearing heavy body armor and carrying weapons, just one of the boys.

"It felt like being part of this brotherhood that you hear about so often when you talk about the military," he said. "It was invaluable."

On Nov. 16, he was put to work just hours after arriving in Afghanistan. During 12-hour night shifts that began at 4 P.M., he was responsible for intercepting communications by militants in order to guide Special Operations troops carrying out missions. For the first time in his career, the intelligence he was gathering was being put to immediate use and resulting in constant expressions of gratitude. Feeling indispensable in a critical job, Wilson started worrying less about being discovered.

"At that point, I had no concerns about it," he said. "I felt confident about my ability to do my job and I was hopeful that would be enough if everything did come out. That that would be enough to stay."

An Early Exit

The secret was exposed in late November when Wilson's commanders in Afghanistan spoke to his superiors in Hawaii to make arrangements for a promotion he was due. Officials in Hawaii used female pronouns to refer to Wilson, while their counterparts at Bagram were referring to a male petty officer third class.

"My Afghanistan leadership was like, 'I have no idea who you are talking about,'" Wilson said. "We don't have a female with that last name. I think you have the wrong shop."

After Wilson came clean, commanders in Afghanistan decided to send him home. Within six hours, he was packed and loaded onto a plane. As the sun rose that morning, his prevailing concern was who would fill his slot inside the ramshackle intelligence fusion cell.

"My main concern was not I could potentially be losing my career, but what about the guys on the ground," he said, noting that there was no one else on base trained to do the job.

On the flight home, he was surrounded by war-weary troops elated about the thought of seeing loved ones back home and indulging in the comforts of life in America. Wilson wanted nothing more than to go back to war.

"I didn't get to say goodbye to anyone," he said. "I have no idea what they told people."

When he arrived in Hawaii a few days later, his commanders promoted him. Weeks later, he received a commendation letter from Vice Admiral Jan E. Tighe, who oversaw his unit. Superiors were respectful and at times seemed apologetic, said Wilson, who recalls a sergeant major telling him: "You know, we are overreacting because we have no idea what to do with you."

After weeks of deliberations, a military lawyer gave Wilson a choice: "You can transition, or you can serve," the sailor said he was told.

That wasn't a choice to Wilson, who soon signed his honorable discharge papers and left Hawaii.

A Navy spokesman said that officials in Wilson's command did not wish to be interviewed about the sailor's ordeal. "Petty Officer Wilson served honorably," Lt. Cmdr. Chris Servello said in an e-mail.

A Pentagon spokeswoman, Lt. Col. Cathy Wilkinson, said the Defense Department does not know how many service members have been discharged for being transgender. She said the Pentagon has no plan to change its medical qualification standards based on the changes to the psychiatric association's entry on gender disorder, but she noted that medical policies are being constantly reviewed.

"In doing these reviews, the department considers that service members must serve in austere environments, many of which make necessary and ongoing treatments related to sex reassignment and many other conditions untenable," she said in an e-mailed statement.

Since he was discharged a month ago, Wilson has been sleeping on an air mattress on the floor of a friend's apartment in Manhattan. Having kept his security clearance, he could easily return to the same line of work for an intelligence agency or even the Pentagon, as a civilian. But he yearns to wear the uniform again.

"The military gave me the backbone to transition, to be who I am, because they look so fondly on honor and courage and all those things you have to have to be fully authentic," he said. "I don't think I would have gotten to where I am today without that."

Periodical and Internet Sources Bibliography

The following articles have been selected to supplement the diverse views presented in this chapter.

Lawrence Bonk	"Is the Pentagon Quietly Reconsidering Its Stance on Transgendered People in the Military?," Independent Journal Review, April 14, 2015.
Tom Vanden Brook	"Carter Says Military Seeks New Ways to Attract Troops," *USA Today*, March 30, 2015.
Juliet Eilperin	"Transgender in the Military: A Pentagon in Transition Weighs Its Policy," *Washington Post*, April 9, 2015.
Teresa Fazio	"Testing a Few Good Women for Combat," *At War* (blog), *New York Times*, March 19, 2015.
Jane Henderson	"Hiding in Plain Sight: Gays in the Military," *St. Louis Post-Dispatch* (Missouri), February 26, 2015.
Chris Johnson	"Army Soldier Becomes First Openly Trans Person in U.S. Military," *Washington Blade*, April 10, 2015.
Bryant Jordan	"Why Experience Will Determine Effects of Women Entering Combat Roles," Military.com, March 19, 2015.
Jim Michaels	"Experimental Force Will Test Marine Women in Combat Roles," *USA Today*, March 12, 2014.
David Scott	"Why the U.S. Needs the Draft," StarNews Online, April 17, 2015.
Leo Shane III	"Why One Lawmaker Keeps Pushing for a New Military Draft," *Military Times*, March 30, 2015.

OPPOSING
VIEWPOINTS®
SERIES

CHAPTER 4

How Is the United States Caring for Its Veterans?

Chapter Preface

For veterans struggling with post-traumatic stress disorder (PTSD), there is an unexpected treatment: dogs. Several programs pair veterans with service dogs. The K9s for Warriors program, for example, is a Florida-based project that places dogs with those suffering from PTSD. The dogs help veterans who experience stress in crowded conditions or who get startled when someone appears from behind suddenly. For example, the dogs can get between veterans and people in front of them or can warn veterans when someone is approaching from their blind sides. "So now I can actually go in a place like that and I just relax, and it doesn't really bother me because I know that she's with me," said Joe Swoboda, a veteran whose service dog, Lilly, offers him comfort after his three tours of duty in Iraq.

As of April 2015, K9s for Warriors had placed more than 160 dogs with veterans and had raised $800,000 for a new kennel; the demand for additional dogs is high and growing, according to a news story from WCSH-6 in Portland, Maine. Unfortunately, that means that there can be a long wait to receive a placement. Veterans first have to have a diagnosis of PTSD; they then have to apply to the program, and if they are accepted, the waiting list for dogs can still be over a year long.

The federal Service Dogs for Veterans Act also places dogs with veterans. Since its inception in 2009, the program has placed two hundred service dogs with veterans. The program is very expensive; training and placement cost about $25,000 for each dog. However, the dogs can be very helpful in mitigating the effects of PTSD. In a May 2015 interview with the Minneapolis *Star Tribune*, Tony Tengwall, a veteran and veterans' service officer, explained how his service dog helps keep him calm. Tengwall was paired with Fitz, a psychiatric service dog, who helps both him and the veterans who visit him for help at the Anoka County Veteran Services. "I haven't had an angry vet since I got Fitz," Tengwall says. "They come in sometimes angry, sit down, and start petting him. And then their mood completely changes." If Tengwall himself is becoming angry or upset, for example while driving, Fitz will put his head on Tengwall's shoulder to remind him to calm down. "I don't realize I'm getting worked up until I look down and see Fitz there," Tengwall says.

Other issues surrounding the well-being of veterans, including the quality of health care they receive and the incidence of post-traumatic stress disorder after combat, are explored in the following chapter.

> *"The VA has a nearly lifelong relation-*
> *ship with most of its patients and does*
> *not profit from their illnesses. This gives*
> *it incentives to keep its patients well."*

Veterans in the United States Receive High-Quality Care

Phillip Longman

Phillip Longman is a senior fellow at the New America Founda-
tion and the author of Best Care Anywhere: Why VA Health
Care Would Be Better for Everyone. *In the following viewpoint,*
he argues that the health care system under the Department of
Veterans Affairs (VA) is vastly superior to civilian health care.
He says that the VA has better oversight and better incentives to
provide quality care. He admits that the VA can be slow to pro-
vide care and that it should be streamlined. He argues, however,
that the quality of the VA medical system is very high and should
be a model for civilian health care.

As you read, consider the following questions:

1. What does Longman say was the inspiration for his
   book on health care?

2. Who does Longman credit with leadership in creating the high-quality VA system?

3. What recommendations does Longman suggest to cut VA waiting times in the future?

I am not a veteran nor a VA [Department of Veterans Affairs] employee. I am also not affiliated with any veterans' service organization. Instead, the perspective I bring comes from my having written a book about the transformation of the VA health care system. The book, now in its third edition, is called *Best Care Anywhere: Why VA Health Care Would Be Better for Everyone.*

The inspiration for the book came from my experience in losing my first wife, Robin, to breast cancer, in 1999.

Robin was treated at a highly renowned cancer center here in Washington, DC. I never blamed her doctors for her death. But suffice it to say that what I saw of this one prestigious corner of the American health care system caused me to become extremely alarmed [at] the problem of medical errors and poorly coordinated care.

Shortly after Robin's death, the Institute of Medicine issued a landmark report in which it estimated that up to 98,000 Americans are killed every year in hospitals as a result of medical errors. That's like three jumbo jets crashing every other day and killing all on board.

Then came another report published in the *Journal of the American Medical Association*, which looked not just at hospitals, but at the American health care system as a whole. It estimated that through a combination of undertreatment, overtreatment, and mistreatment, the U.S. health care system is killing 225,000 Americans per year. To put that in perspective, it means that contact with the U.S. health system is the third-largest cause of death in the United States, following all heart disease and all cancers.

These reports, combined with my personal experience, put me on a quest to find out who had the best workable solutions to America's dysfunctional and dangerous health care delivery system.

VA as a Model

The answer that emerged was not one I expected. But as study after study now confirms, the VA system as a whole outperforms the rest of the health care system on just about every metric that health care quality experts can devise. These include adherence to the protocols of evidence-based medicine, investment in prevention and effective disease management, use of integrated electronic medical records, and, importantly, patient satisfaction.

Just how the VA transformed itself is an inspiring story, involving frontline employees bringing about a revolution from below, as well as courageous leadership at the top, particularly during the period when Dr. Kenneth Kizer headed the Veterans Health Administration.

As I also explain in my book, important structural factors were at work as well. For example, the VA has a nearly lifelong relationship with most of its patients and does not profit from their illnesses. This gives it incentives to keep its patients well—incentives that are sorely lacking in most of the rest of the health care system. If the VA doesn't teach its patient how to effectively manage their diabetes, for example, it becomes liable down the line for the cost of their amputations, renal failures, and all the other long-term complications of the disease.

Now, of course, bad medicine does happen at the VA, and when it does those who may be responsible need to be thoroughly investigated. But when such breakdowns occur, we should always put them in context by asking: "Compared to what?"

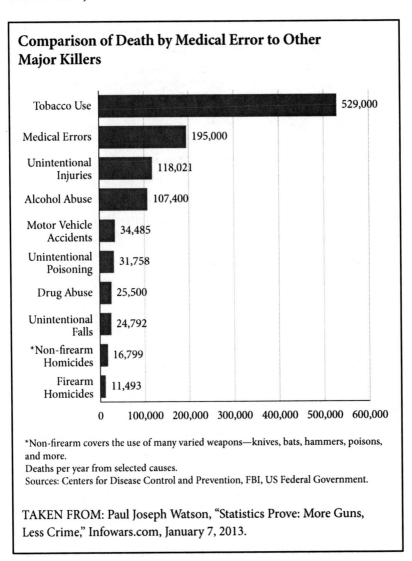

Comparison of Death by Medical Error to Other Major Killers

Cause	Deaths
Tobacco Use	529,000
Medical Errors	195,000
Unintentional Injuries	118,021
Alcohol Abuse	107,400
Motor Vehicle Accidents	34,485
Unintentional Poisoning	31,758
Drug Abuse	25,500
Unintentional Falls	24,792
*Non-firearm Homicides	16,799
Firearm Homicides	11,493

*Non-firearm covers the use of many varied weapons—knives, bats, hammers, poisons, and more.
Deaths per year from selected causes.
Sources: Centers for Disease Control and Prevention, FBI, US Federal Government.

TAKEN FROM: Paul Joseph Watson, "Statistics Prove: More Guns, Less Crime," Infowars.com, January 7, 2013.

As we've seen, U.S. health care outside of the VA is exceptionally dangerous. It would have been great, for example, if the private hospital that treated my wife had been under the scrutiny of an Inspector General [IG], whose full-time job it was to look out for failures in patient care. But of course, private hospitals don't have IGs.

Similarly, if a committee of Congress such as this one [U.S. Senate Committee on Veterans' Affairs] was specifically focused on the quality of care provided by that hospital, that oversight would have likely helped the institution to become more accountable. Or again, more mistakes would undoubtedly have come to light at that hospital and many others if effective watchdog group akin to the American Legion looked out for the interest of non-VA patients.

But, of course, that kind of scrutiny does not occur. And this asymmetry creates a perverse result. For the average news consumer it can lead to the impression that the VA is limping along from one scandal to the next, even as its patients and health care quality experts applaud its superior quality, safety, and cost-effectiveness.

Care vs. Waiting Time

Finally, I'll close by pointing out another way in which context is often missing in discussion of VA health care. Overwhelmingly, the failures of the VA in recent years haven't been about the quality of health care for those who get covered. Instead, they've mostly been about the excessive waiting times and excessive red tape that our vets must go through to establish eligibility.

Here, the Veterans Benefits Administration must accept blame for not doing a better job of streamlining administrative procedures. But in all fairness, it is Congress, and by extension the American people as a whole, who have established the laws that require most vets to prove that they have service-related disabilities before becoming eligible for VA care.

This is the perverse root cause of the waiting time and other problems of access. Who can say if a Vietnam vet is losing his hearing due to exposure to too much artillery fire or exposure to too many Who concerts? [The Who is a 1960s British rock band.]

We need to open up the VA and grow it, extending no-questions-asked eligibility not only to all vets but to their family members as well. This not only makes clinical sense; it also makes economic sense. So long as the VA remains one of, if not the most, cost-effective, scientifically driven, integrated health care delivery systems in the country, the more patients it treats, the better for everyone.

> "*The Veterans Health Administration ... has systematically ignored warnings about its deficiencies and must be fundamentally restructured.*"

The US Veteran Health Care System Is Overwhelmed and Failing

Associated Press

The Associated Press is a news service. In the following viewpoint, it reports on a review of health care administered under the Department of Veterans Affairs (VA). The review found long delays in care for veterans and a lack of accountability. The review recommended sweeping changes, including more resources for the VA health system. The Veterans Health Administration was especially troubled and inefficient, the review found.

As you read, consider the following questions:

1. According to the viewpoint, who is Rob Nabors, and what was his involvement in veterans' affairs?

2. Which of the review's recommendations does the author say will likely face skepticism among Republicans?

3. What changes in demographic profiles of veterans does the review say the VA needs to prepare for, according to the viewpoint?

Citing "significant and chronic system failures" in the nation's health system for veterans, a review ordered by President Barack Obama portrays the Department of Veterans Affairs [VA] as a struggling agency battling a corrosive culture of distrust, lacking in resources and ill-prepared to deal with an influx of new and older veterans with a range of medical and mental health care needs.

Restructuring Necessary

The scathing report by deputy White House chief of staff Rob Nabors says the Veterans Health Administration [VHA], the VA sub-agency that provides health care to about 8.8 million veterans a year, has systematically ignored warnings about its deficiencies and must be fundamentally restructured.

Obama ordered the review last month [in May 2014] in a response to widespread reports of long delays for treatment and medical appointments and of veterans dying while on waiting lists. But Nabors's report goes far beyond the lengthy waits and manipulated schedules raised by whistle-blowers and chronicled in past internal and congressional investigations.

The review offers a series of recommendations, including a need for more doctors, nurses and trained administrative staff—proposals that are likely to face skepticism among some congressional Republicans who have blamed the VA's problems on mismanagement, not lack of resources.

"We know that unacceptable, systemic problems and cultural issues within our health system prevent veterans from receiving timely care," acting VA secretary Sloan Gibson said in a statement following an Oval Office meeting Friday with Obama and Nabors. "We can and must solve these problems as we work to earn back the trust of veterans."

Problems at the VHA

While the review finds deficiencies throughout the VA, it is especially critical of the Veterans Health Administration, which has already undergone some housecleaning. Earlier this week, the VA announced that Dr. Robert Jesse, who has been acting undersecretary for health and head of the VHA, was resigning. Jesse has been acting undersecretary for health since May 16 [2014], when Robert Petzel resigned under pressure months before he was set to retire.

Nabors's report found that the VHA, the country's biggest health care system, acts with little transparency or accountability and many recommendations to improve care are slowly implemented or ignored. The report says concerns raised by the public, monitors or even VA leadership have been dismissed at the VHA as "exaggerated, unimportant, or 'will pass.'"

Among Nabors's other findings:

- As of June 23, the independent Office of Special Counsel, a government investigative arm, had more than 50 pending cases that allege threats to patient health or safety.

- One-fourth of all the whistle-blower cases under review across the federal government come from the VA. The department "encourages discontent and backlash against employees."

- The VA's lack of resources reflects troubles in the health care field as a whole and in the federal government. But the VA has been unable to connect its budget needs to specific outcomes.

- The VA needs to better prepare for changes in the demographic profile of veterans, including more female veterans, a surge in mental health needs and a growing number of older veterans.

"No organization the size of VA can operate effectively without a high level of transparency and accountability," said Sen. Bernie Sanders, the Vermont independent who heads the Senate's Veterans' Affairs Committee. "Clearly that is not the case now at the VA."

Obama asked Nabors to stay at the VA temporarily to continue to provide assistance.

The White House said that over the past month, the VA has contacted 135,000 veterans and scheduled about 182,000 additional appointments. It has also used more mobile medical units to attend to veterans awaiting care.

Since reports surfaced of treatment delays and of patients dying while on waiting lists, the VA has been the subject of internal, independent and congressional investigations. The VA has confirmed that dozens of veterans died while awaiting appointments at VA facilities in the Phoenix area, although officials say it's unclear whether the delays were the cause of the deaths.

One VA audit found that 10% of veterans seeking medical care at VA hospitals and clinics have to wait at least 30 days for an appointment. More than 56,000 veterans have had to wait at least three months for initial appointments, according to the report, and an additional 46,000 veterans who asked for appointments over the past decade never got them.

*"This smacks of a cover-up to avoid li-
ability for a disgraceful policy that deprived our nation's veterans of appropriate health care."*

Post-Traumatic Stress Disorder Is Underdiagnosed

Mary Susan Littlepage

*Mary Susan Littlepage is a writer for Truthout, a progressive
news organization. In the following viewpoint, she reports that
an ethics organization has filed a request for Department of Veterans Affairs (VA) documents pertaining to post-traumatic stress
disorder (PTSD). The VA says it destroyed the documents. Littlepage writes that this is disturbing because of concerns that the
VA has been underdiagnosing PTSD and thereby preventing veterans from receiving needed mental health care and benefits.*

As you read, consider the following questions:

1. According to Littlepage, who is Norma Perez, and why is
   she important to the effort to uncover underdiagnosing
   of PTSD?

2. The viewpoint suggests that the military underdiagnosed
   PTSD during what period?

3. According to the viewpoint, why does John Livornese say the VA does not have the e-mails requested in the Freedom of Information Act request?

The Citizens for Responsibility and Ethics in Washington (CREW) filed a lawsuit against the Department of Veterans Affairs (VA) after the VA admitted to destroying documents responding to CREW's May 2008 Freedom of Information [Act] (FOIA) request. CREW's FOIA request called for documents related to the VA's policy of underdiagnosing posttraumatic stress disorder (PTSD).

Destruction of Records

CREW learned of the underdiagnosing of PTSD after learning of an e-mail in which VA employee Norma Perez discussed the policy. According to CREW, the VA has resisted providing any documents; it stated that the VA claimed it had produced everything it had, even though it hasn't turned over the Perez e-mail or any other records referring to the e-mail.

Therefore, CREW has argued that the VA's search for documents has been inadequate, and the VA has argued that it destroyed in 2008 many e-mails and backup tapes, which included the Perez e-mail. The VA has contended that it cannot produce any e-mails before December 9, 2008.

Anne Weismann, CREW's chief counsel, said, "There appears to be—and I don't know this for certain—a growing recognition on the part of the VA that there has been an underdiagnosis [of PTSD] and there seems to be a growing recognition that they have a problem with high suicide rates. Obviously recognizing there is a problem is the first step toward curing it, but that's why the actions of the VA here in destroying e-mails is so disturbing."

What CREW hopes to achieve with the lawsuit is to get records that would confirm the extent to which there is an underdiagnosis of PTSD that's underreported, she said.

"We don't think we have all the records, and now we know that some of the key records were destroyed," she said. "I can't really speak definitively on the scope of the problem because we don't have all the records yet. Most critically we're missing some key documents surrounding this one e-mail, which we have not because the VA gave it to us but because someone in the organization bravely decided to leak it."

In addition, Weismann said, "It is incredible that with all of the public outrage and concern over this issue, the VA took no steps to preserve important records. This smacks of a cover-up to avoid liability for a disgraceful policy that deprived our nation's veterans of appropriate health care."

Also, Weismann said, "The VA is not above the law; like all other agencies, it cannot simply destroy documents that have been requested under the FOIA just because those documents may cast the agency in a bad light."

Denied Benefits

In the brief, Weismann and Daniel S. Alcorn, counsel for CREW, stated that recent news reports indicate that thousands of veterans discharged from military service with PTSD between 2002 and 2008 are now eligible to have their disability status reviewed on an expedited basis.

The military has agreed to expedite these reviews in response to a class-action lawsuit filed by seven combat veterans, who allege that the military illegally denied benefits to those discharged because of PTSD over a six-year period that ended October 14, 2008. "It is clear from these news reports that during the period 2002 to 2008—a period covered by CREW's FOIA request—there was a widespread underdiagnosis of PTSD among U.S. military service personnel affecting thousands of discharged veterans," the brief stated.

Also, the brief stated that it is "apparent [that] the VA has not made an adequate search and release of records responsive to CREW's request." That's because the VA admitted "it pur-

What Is Post-Traumatic Stress Disorder (PTSD)?

When in danger, it's natural to feel afraid. This fear triggers many split-second changes in the body to prepare to defend against the danger or to avoid it. This "fight-or-flight" response is a healthy reaction meant to protect a person from harm. But in post-traumatic stress disorder (PTSD), this reaction is changed or damaged. People who have PTSD may feel stressed or frightened even when they're no longer in danger.

PTSD develops after a terrifying ordeal that involved physical harm or the threat of physical harm. The person who develops PTSD may have been the one who was harmed, the harm may have happened to a loved one, or the person may have witnessed a harmful event that happened to loved ones or strangers.

PTSD was first brought to public attention in relation to war veterans, but it can result from a variety of traumatic incidents, such as mugging, rape, torture, being kidnapped or held captive, child abuse, car accidents, train wrecks, plane crashes, bombings, or natural disasters such as floods or earthquakes.

National Institute of Mental Health,
"Post-Traumatic Stress Disorder (PTSD)."

posefully destroyed responsive records during the pendency of CREW's FOIA request and this lawsuit."

In trying to account for the VA's failure to locate the Perez e-mail central to the case, John Livornese, director of the FOIA Service of the Department of Veterans Affairs, said that the VA has no e-mail history for Perez prior to December 9, 2008, because the back-up tapes for the entire system containing the Perez e-mails were reused and all data on those tapes was rewritten, according to the brief.

"In other words, the VA destroyed potentially responsive records after CREW made its FOIA request in this matter on May 14, 2008—a request that expressly sought e-mails and other electronic records—and after CREW filed its lawsuit on August 27, 2008, in this case," the brief stated.

The brief called for the court to direct the VA to conduct additional searches, including of the e-mail accounts of all VA employees, to find responsive records.

In the brief, Weismann and Alcorn argued that an agency is not permitted to destroy responsive records once they have been requested under the FOIA request: "An agency's intentional destruction of a document requested under the FOIA bears on the issue of whether the agency conducted an adequate search. That is because whatever search the agency did conduct 'would not be reasonably calculated to uncover all relevant documents,' as the FOIA requires."

New Searches

Weismann and Alcorn call for the VA to be required to try to reconstruct the destroyed records or information contained in the restored records. "Although the 2008 Perez e-mail has been destroyed from the back-up tapes on which it was stored, the e-mail and other relevant documents and information may still reside on computer hard drives at the worksite for Ms. Perez or in hard files at that site," they stated.

In addition, the pair call for the VA to make "adequate searches for responsive records for release to CREW" because of the recent reports that thousands of veterans discharged with PTSD from 2002 to 2008 may have been denied benefits due to underscoring in a rating system used to determine benefits.

In conclusion, CREW "requests that the court order the VA to conduct renewed and broader searches and provide

CREW with all responsive records not yet produced." CREW also calls for the court to hold a hearing on the issue of document destruction and to require the VA to account for its actions.

| *"The crazed, strung-out vet is exactly the image we are trying to dispel."*

Public Stereotypes That All Veterans Have PTSD Are Harmful

Sally Satel and Richard J. McNally

Sally Satel is a practicing psychiatrist and resident scholar at the American Enterprise Institute for Public Policy Research. Richard J. McNally is a professor of psychology at Harvard University and the author of What Is Mental Illness? *In the following viewpoint, they argue that the stereotype that all veterans suffer from post-traumatic stress disorder can be harmful to veterans. Veterans, they say, are not typically mentally ill or dangerous. The majority are happy with their service and positive about returning to civilian life. The authors conclude that most veterans do well if they can find jobs and are able to find outlets to talk about their experiences.*

As you read, consider the following questions:

1. How did films such as *Rambo* portray veterans, according to the authors?

2. What do the authors argue is the single most important key to easing financial stress and other problems for veterans?

3. What do the authors report as the risk factors for veteran suicides?

In the early 1970s, a group of antiwar psychiatrists, most prominently Robert Jay Lifton, renowned for his work on the traumatic impact of Hiroshima, became concerned about the corrosive effect of the Vietnam War on the minds of the men who fought it. As Lifton told a Senate committee in 1970, the veteran "returns as a tainted intruder ... likely to seek continuing outlets for a pattern of violence to which they have become habituated." To Lifton, the process of readjustment was one of "rehumanization."

Rambo Is Not Reality

The stereotype of the mentally scarred vet that seized the public imagination during the Vietnam conflict lingers to this day, in part due to the media's infatuation with the theme. Films such as *Taxi Driver*, *Rambo*, and *Coming Home* portrayed the veteran as a "walking time bomb." Print media told much the same story. In 1972, the *New York Times* ran a front-page story, "Postwar Shock Is Found to Beset Veterans Returning from the War in Vietnam," reporting that half of all Vietnam veterans were "psychiatric casualties of war" in need of "professional help to readjust."

Today, according to a 2012 poll conducted by Greenberg Quinlan Rosner Research, over half of the public believes that the majority of post-9/11 [referring to September 11, 2001] veterans suffer from post-traumatic stress disorder. It's a belief that could be hindering, rather than helping, service members returning home from Afghanistan and Iraq.

What did Vietnam veterans say about themselves? A large 1980 Harris poll conducted for the House Committee on

Veterans' Affairs revealed that 90 percent said that, "looking back," they were either "very glad" or "somewhat glad" to have "served their country." Eighty percent said that returning home was "about the same or better" than they had "anticipated." In short, said the pollster's report, many respondents rejected "sensationalist exaggeration [which bears] little resemblance to the experiences and present realities of the emotional lives of these veterans," according to the report.

Mostly, veterans said they felt invisible, anonymous, and ignored by the public. Former combat Marine and future U.S. senator James H. Webb observed in 1976 how the men who fought in Vietnam "traditionally lacked access to the media and the power centers of this country."

In a 1981 *National Journal* article, Jonathan Rauch quoted Bobby Muller, the head of Vietnam Veterans of America [Foundation]: "The crazed, strung-out vet is exactly the image we are trying to dispel."

But these images and perspectives were largely obscured.

Today, the voices of veterans of the post-9/11 wars are coming through loud and clear, thanks to a variety of non-profits, as well as the outreach efforts and blogs of the veterans themselves.

Lt. Col. Daniel Gade, now an assistant professor of political science at the U.S. Military Academy at West Point, lost a leg and nearly his life fighting in Iraq. He has recovered, but he's concerned about his fellow veterans. Too often, Gade recently wrote at *National Affairs*, the emphasis from well-meaning helpers is "on what an injured soldier is *not* able to do [rather] than on increasing what he *is* able to do." And *doing*, Gade makes clear, is the powerful engine behind a successful transition to civilian life.

David Eisler, who served in Iraq and Afghanistan and is now a graduate student at Columbia University, cautions in the *New York Times* about "eye-catching headlines about post-traumatic stress disorder and difficulties readjusting to civilian

Veterans and Unemployment

Problems of unemployment and underemployment, which are broadly felt by the US civilian population today, appear to be more acute for veterans of the post-9/11 era, particularly young veterans. In 2011, the employment rate among all post-9/11 veterans 18 years old and older was more than one-third higher than that among equivalent nonveterans—12.1% compared with 8.7%. Among veterans 18–24 years old, the rate was almost twice as high—30.2% compared with 16.1%. The sources of those disparities remain unclear and could include skills mismatch, impeded ability to maintain or obtain employment because of physical- or mental-health trauma, stigma or discrimination, or some combination of those factors or other elements. Successful readjustment depends on reentry into the civilian workforce, and the available evidence suggests that this is an important gap for policy to address. The committee found that the literature assessing the effectiveness of DOD's [Department of Defense's] and VA's [Department of Veterans Affairs'] transition-assistance programs is relatively thin, even though reentry into the labor force is one of the most important readjustment challenges.

Institute of Medicine of the National Academies,
Returning Home from Iraq and Afghanistan:
Assessment of Readjustment Needs of Veterans,
Service Members, and Their Families. Washington DC:
National Academics Press, 2013, pp. 7–8

life after years of war." It's more nuanced than that. "It's surely possible," he later wrote to us, "for a veteran to be an asset to a corporation or as a public servant, even if he also required some degree of care and attention outside work."

Work as Care

In fact, though, one of the most important forms of care a veteran can receive is the work itself. Based upon our experience with patients, work is the single most effective key to easing financial stress, marital tensions, and the void of loneliness. Unfortunately, unemployment among veterans from the Iraq and Afghanistan Wars is almost 10 percent, above the national average. On November 6, [100,000] Jobs Mission, a consortium of over 100 private companies, announced plans to find 200,000 positions for veterans and military spouses by 2020. Their efforts complement campaigns by the White House and U.S. Chamber of Commerce.

A sense of engagement in the community is also vital, and while employment contributes to engagement, another component involves the sharing of experiences. "The process of communicating a personal war experience to a formal or public audience serves a critical role in the readjustment of the veteran," wrote anthropologist Don Gomez, a two-tour Iraq War veteran, in 2011 at *Small Wars Journal*, a site founded by former Marines. This is an area where blogs and nonprofits— like *Small Wars Journal*—have been particularly effective. (Gomez himself believes that he has benefited from being able to "share my war experience through public writing.") Another nonprofit outfit, the Mission Continues, engages veterans in projects that "bridge the military-civilian divide, allowing veterans to feel more connected to their communities and helping civilians gain a better understanding of and appreciation for our men and women in uniform."

Though the post-9/11 narrative of reengagement is more optimistic than its Vietnam counterpart, there's no doubt that the "after war," as journalist David Finkel has called it, can go terribly wrong for a small minority, as the reports of suicide in veterans attest. The question is how to interpret the numbers: Who is committing suicide, and for what reasons?

The Department of Veterans Affairs puts the numbers of veterans who die by suicide at between 18–22 per day. While the percentage of all suicides nationwide reported as "veteran" has decreased since 2000, the absolute number of suicides by veterans has increased. Yet over half of the veterans who died by suicide last year were over 50 years of age; far fewer were from the post-9/11 cohort.

Suicide Not Rooted in PTSD

Contrary to expectation, the roots of suicide do not appear to lie in the number or extent of deployments, exposure to combat, or to PTSD itself, as data from the massive US Millennium Cohort Study indicate.

In fact, according to a study featured in the *Journal of the American Medical Association* in 2013, over half of all active-duty personnel who died by suicide between July 2001 and December 2008 were never deployed to Iraq and Afghanistan, and 77 percent of all personnel who died by suicide never saw combat. Instead, the data point to other risk factors, such as mood disorders and alcohol problems. Further factors surely play a role in suicide as well: Financial pressure—exacerbated by recent economic disruption—marital discord, and social isolation, often mixed with alcohol, can be lethal.

War veterans have always faced readjustment problems. The newer generation of veterans does not speak as one, of course, but there are eloquent commonalities in their stories. They don't downplay the devastation and moral ambiguities of their experience as they seek to connect through writing, teaching, and work. Instead of being told "you couldn't understand, you weren't there," a time-honored way of keeping others at a distance, we're more apt to hear from people like Gade, Eisler, and Gomez, "let us tell you." The telling, it turns out, is important.

Periodical and Internet Sources Bibliography

The following articles have been selected to supplement the diverse views presented in this chapter.

Brent Budowsky	"How to Save the Lives of Troubled Vets," *The Hill*, September 4, 2014.
Molly Joel Coye	"Nearly Half of Veterans Who Seek Help Receive Inadequate Care," *The Hill*, February 9, 2015.
Thomas Gibbons-Neff	"Haunted by Their Decisions in War," *Washington Post*, March 6, 2015.
Michelle Ye Hee Lee	"The Missing Context Behind the Widely Cited Statistic That There Are 22 Veteran Suicides a Day," *Washington Post*, February 4, 2015.
Bobby Liga	"1 in 3 Returning Military Members Have PTSD, Experts Say," Live5News.com, April 3, 2015.
Clare Roth and Ben Kieffer	"Eliminating Barriers to Mental Health Care for Veterans," Iowa Public Radio, April 10, 2015.
Dennis Wagner	"Veterans Propose Major Changes in VA Health Care," *USA Today*, February 26, 2015.
Dennis Wagner	"A Year Later: VA Struggles to Improve Care Nationwide," AZCentral.com, April 10, 2015.
Adam Zarembo	"Detailed Study Confirms High Suicide Rate Among Recent Veterans," *Los Angeles Times*, January 14, 2015.
Gregg Zoroya	"Army Chaplains Need Training to Help Suicidal Soldiers," *USA Today*, April 7, 2015.

For Further Discussion

Chapter 1

1. In his viewpoint, Scott Rasmussen quotes Ronald Reagan, who said, "Defense is not a budget issue. You spend what you need." How does Rasmussen use that statement to justify reducing the defense budget in the twenty-first century? Do you agree with Rasmussen's argument? Explain your reasoning.

2. Jon Basil Utley argues that sequestration, or across-the-board spending cuts, are a good way to reduce waste in defense spending and develop more sound policy when it comes to defense. He provides eight suggestions on how sequestration can help policy makers determine where budget cuts can be made. Choose two of the eight suggestions and elaborate on why you think these suggestions will or will not be effective in reducing the military's budget.

3. Robert B. Reich argues that having a huge undercover military jobs program is not a good way to keep Americans employed. He says that it creates jobs the United States really doesn't need. What does he propose, instead of making obsolete weapons systems and unnecessary military equipment? Do you agree or disagree with Reich's argument? Explain your reasoning.

Chapter 2

1. In his viewpoint, Peter Dizikes points out that political scientist Barry Posen believes there are three main points that should guide US foreign policy and military deployment. What are those three points? Which do you think

should be the main driving factor that determines whether the United States interferes in world affairs? Explain your reasoning.

2. Jorge Benitez argues that the United States and other Western countries should intervene in Ukraine to stop Russian aggression in other countries. Doug Bandow argues that the United States should stay out of the Russia-Ukraine dispute for numerous reasons, chief among them that Russian relations with the United States are more important than Ukrainian-US relations. With which author do you agree more? Explain your reasoning, using text from the viewpoint to support your answer.

Chapter 3

1. Thom Serafin argues that the United States should bring back the draft to give Americans a greater stake in decisions on foreign policy and military deployment that Serafin feels can no longer be entrusted solely to Washington policy makers. Do you think that bringing back the draft would make the government less likely to use military intervention? Why, or why not?

2. Patrick J. Buchanan argues that women should not serve in combat roles in the US military. He offers a comparison between athletics and the military, arguing that women are not allowed to play on men's football, basketball, baseball, hockey, or lacrosse teams, yet they are allowed to fight alongside men in the battlefield. Do you think that Buchanan makes a legitimate argument with this example? Why, or why not?

3. The policy known as Don't Ask, Don't Tell, which prohibited gay, lesbian, and bisexual people from serving openly in the military, was repealed in 2011. However, the repeal did not apply to transgender individuals who wish to join the US military. Such individuals still are prohibited from joining the armed forces if their transgender status is

known. In your opinion, do you think transgender individuals should be allowed to serve openly in the US military? Why, or why not?

Chapter 4

1. Phillip Longman argues that the VA health system outperforms the rest of the American health care system, even
though VA patients might experience longer wait times
and more bureaucratic red tape. The Associated Press reported on an evaluation of the VA health care system that
recommended several changes be made to improve the
system. After reading both viewpoints, what is your assessment of VA health care in the United States? Do you
think improvements are necessary? Explain.

2. Sally Satel and Richard J. McNally report in their viewpoint that employment is the single most effective key to
easing financial stress, marital tensions, and the loneliness
of veterans. However, unemployment among veterans
from the Iraq and Afghanistan Wars is almost 10 percent
above the national average. Do you think that the perception that post-9/11 veterans are suffering from post-
traumatic stress disorder contributes to this high rate of
unemployment? What do you think are other contributing
factors to veteran unemployment? Explain.

Organizations to Contact

The editors have compiled the following list of organizations concerned with the issues debated in this book. The descriptions are derived from materials provided by the organizations. All have publications or information available for interested readers. The list was compiled on the date of publication of the present volume; the information provided here may change. Be aware that many organizations take several weeks or longer to respond to inquiries, so allow as much time as possible.

American Legion
700 N. Pennsylvania Street, PO Box 1055
Indianapolis, IN   46206
(317) 630-1200 • fax: (317) 630-1223
website: www.legion.org

Established in 1919, the American Legion is the nation's largest veterans' service organization. It provides a number of services to US veterans and their communities, including mentoring kids and sponsoring youth programs; advocating for a strong national security; and supporting policies and programs that help American service members and veterans. The American Legion is particularly political, actively lobbying for pro-military and pro-veterans policies. It offers a wide range of publications, including the *American Legion Magazine*, annual reports, brochures, and handbooks. Its website provides access to the *Burn Pit* blog.

American Veterans (AMVETS)
4647 Forbes Boulevard, Lanham, MD   20706-4380
(301) 459-9600 • fax: (301) 459-7924
e-mail: amvets@amvets.org
website: www.amvets.org

With more than 250,000 members, American Veterans (AMVETS) is one of the leading veterans' service organizations in the United States. It stands as a strong and influential advocate for America's veterans on important issues such as employment and training, mandatory funding for government-provided health care, and other benefits to which veterans are entitled. AMVETS lobbies for effective national defense policies, services for homeless veterans, adequate funding for the Department of Veterans Affairs (VA), and improved employment and training programs for veterans. It publishes *American Veteran* quarterly magazine, which explores issues relevant to both active-duty military members and veterans.

Center for Security Policy

1901 Pennsylvania Avenue NW, Suite 201
Washington, DC   20006
(202) 835-9077
e-mail: info@securefreedom.org
website: www.centerforsecuritypolicy.org

Based in Washington, DC, the Center for Security Policy is a nonprofit, nonpartisan, national security think tank. It uses diplomatic, informational, military, and economic strength to help establish successful national security policies. Its "Peace Through Strength" philosophy holds that America's national power must be preserved and properly used to enable global peace and stability. The center's website features articles, op-eds, press releases, and transcripts of congressional testimony, as well as the *Free Fire Blog*, which offers entries such as "De-Sexualize the US Military."

Center for Strategic and International Studies (CSIS)

1616 Rhode Island Avenue NW, Washington, DC   20036
(202) 887-0200 • fax: (202) 775-3199
website: www.csis.org

The Center for Strategic and International Studies (CSIS) is a public policy research organization that specializes in US domestic and foreign policy, national security, and economic policy. CSIS analyzes world crisis situations and recommends US military and defense policies. CSIS publishes books, newsletters, and commentaries targeted at decision makers in policy, government, business, and academia. It also publishes the *New Perspectives in Foreign Policy* journal. Its website has a searchable database of news, articles, testimony, and reports, including "The Mindless Debate over Future U.S. Military Manpower in Afghanistan" and "American Military Culture in the Twenty-First Century."

Committee Opposed to Militarism and the Draft (COMD)

PO Box 15195, San Diego, CA 92175
(760) 753-7518
e-mail: comd@comdsd.org
website: www.comdsd.org

The Committee Opposed to Militarism and the Draft (COMD) is an anti-militarism organization "that also challenges the institution of the military, its effect on society, its budget, its role abroad and at home, and the racism, sexism and homophobia that are inherent in the armed forces and Selective Service System." It directs its focus on community education, youth outreach, and direct action. It publishes the quarterly newsletter *Draft NOtices*, which features articles such as "Legal Changes in Military Sexual Assault" and "Attempt to Link Draft Registration to Drivers' Licenses Fails (Again) in California."

Council on Foreign Relations (CFR)

The Harold Pratt House, 58 East Sixty-Eighth Street
New York, NY 10065
(212) 434-9400 • fax: (212) 434-9800
e-mail: communications@cfr.org
website: www.cfr.org

Founded in 1921, the Council on Foreign Relations (CFR) is an independent, nonpartisan membership organization, think tank, and publisher that focuses on foreign policy and international affairs. CFR's mission is to be a resource for its forty-nine hundred members, government officials, business executives, journalists, educators and students, civic and religious leaders, and others to help them better understand the foreign policy choices facing the United States and other nations. CFR has numerous resources available at its website, including backgrounders, interviews, op-eds, videos, podcasts, expert briefs, and blogs. It publishes the bimonthly journal *Foreign Affairs*, which features articles such as "The Future of U.S. Military Power" and "Why the U.S. Army Needs Armor."

Selective Service System

Public and Intergovernmental Affairs, Selective Service System
National Headquarters, Arlington, VA   22209-2425
800-877-8339 • fax: (703) 605-4106
e-mail: information@sss.gov
website: www.sss.gov

The Selective Service System is a small, independent federal agency within the executive branch of the US government that operates with permanent authorization under the Military Selective Service Act. It exists to serve the emergency manpower needs of the military by conscripting untrained men, or personnel with professional health care skills, if directed by Congress and the president because of a national crisis. Federal law requires virtually all men in the United States to register with Selective Service within thirty days of reaching age eighteen. By registering with Selective Service, every young man is reminded of his potential civic obligation to serve the nation in an emergency. Its website offers reports, fast facts, archives of the *Register* newsletter, and information on how to register with Selective Service.

Service Women's Action Network (SWAN)

121 Avenue of the Americas, 6th Floor, New York, NY   10013
(646) 569-5200
e-mail: info@servicewomen.org
website: www.servicewomen.org

The Service Women's Action Network (SWAN) is a nonprofit civil rights organization with a mission to improve the welfare of US servicewomen and female veterans. SWAN works to educate policy makers and legislators; engage military and veteran leadership; organize service members, veterans, and families to build community support; and build coalitions with social justice organizations. SWAN believes that the most effective military is one in which women are integrated into all sectors. SWAN advocates for one single physical fitness standard for both men and women and for occupational standards that are task oriented and gender neutral. SWAN's website provides links to articles such as "Sexual Assault Reports Increase at Naval Academy" and "Women to Participate for First Time in Army Ranger Course."

US Department of Defense (DOD)

1400 Defense Pentagon, Washington, DC   20301-1400
(703) 571-3343
website: www.defense.gov

Headquartered at the Pentagon, the US Department of Defense (DOD) is a governmental agency that provides the military forces needed to deter war and to protect the security of the United States. It is the federal department that supervises all agencies of the government related to national security and the armed forces. The DOD website offers press releases, transcripts, speeches, reports, and articles such as "DOD Seeks Right Standards, Policies for Women in Combat Roles."

US Department of Veterans Affairs (VA)

810 Vermont Avenue NW, Washington, DC   20420
(800) 827-1000
website: www.va.gov

The US Department of Veterans Affairs (VA) is the governmental department that coordinates and administers veterans' programs, including health services, disability compensation, educational and vocational programs, home loans, life insurance, survivors' benefits, and burial remuneration. One of its most important responsibilities is the VA health system, which supervises facilities that offer a wide range of medical, surgical, and rehabilitative care for veterans. The VA website pro-

vides a link to recent congressional testimony, speeches, brochures, fact sheets, and reports. The VA publishes *VAnguard*, a
bimonthly magazine that explores issues relevant to veterans.

Bibliography of Books

Agha Humayun
Amin

Anatomy of US Military's Strategic and Operational Failure in Afghanistan. Seattle, WA: CreateSpace, 2014.

Anders Åslund

Ukraine: What Went Wrong and How to Fix It. Washington, DC: Peterson Institute for International Economics, 2015.

Michael A.
Bellesiles

A People's History of the U.S. Military: Ordinary Soldiers Reflect on Their Experience of War, from the American Revolution to Afghanistan. New York: The New Press, 2013.

Tanya Biank

Undaunted: The Real Story of America's Servicewomen in Today's Military. New York: NAL Caliber, 2014.

Elgin Medea
Brunner

Foreign Security Policy, Gender, and US Military Identity. New York: Palgrave Macmillan, 2013.

Michael J. Butler

Selling a 'Just' War: Framing, Legitimacy, and US Military Intervention. New York: Palgrave Macmillan, 2012.

Kenneth C. Davis

The Hidden History of America at War: Untold Tales from Yorktown to Fallujah. New York: Hachette Books, 2015.

Antulio J. Echevarria II	*Reconsidering the American Way of War: US Military Practice from the Revolution to Afghanistan.* Washington, DC: Georgetown University Press, 2014.
Erin P. Finley	*Fields of Combat: Understanding PTSD Among Veterans of Iraq and Afghanistan.* New York: Cornell University Press, 2011.
Geoffrey Gresh	*Gulf Security and the U.S. Military: Regime Survival and the Politics of Basing.* Stanford, CA: Stanford University Press, 2015.
Steven W. Hook	*US Foreign Policy: The Paradox of World Power.* 4th Ed. Thousand Oaks, CA: CQ Press, 2013.
Brett Jones	*Pride: The Story of the First Openly Gay Navy SEAL.* Indianapolis, IN: Dog Ear Publishing, 2014.
Tim Kane	*Bleeding Talent: How the US Military Mismanages Great Leaders and Why It's Time for a Revolution.* New York: Palgrave Macmillan, 2012.
Joshua E. Kastenberg	*Shaping US Military Law: Governing a Constitutional Military.* Burlington, VT: Ashgate, 2014.
Matt Kennard	*Irregular Army: How the US Military Recruited Neo-Nazis, Gang Members, and Criminals to Fight the War on Terror.* Brooklyn, NY: Verso, 2012.

Nicholas Kerton-Johnson — *Justifying America's Wars: The Conduct and Practice of US Military Intervention*. New York: Routledge, 2012.

John M. Kinder — *Paying with Their Bodies: American War and the Problem of the Disabled Veteran*. Chicago, IL: University of Chicago Press, 2015.

James H. Lebovic — *The Limits of U.S. Military Capability: Lessons from Vietnam and Iraq*. Baltimore, MD: Johns Hopkins University Press, 2010.

Phillip Longman — *Best Care Anywhere: Why VA Health Care Would Be Better for Everyone*. San Francisco, CA: Berrett-Koehler Publishers, 2012.

Megan MacKenzie — *Beyond the Band of Brothers: The US Military and the Myth That Women Can't Fight*. New York: Cambridge University Press, 2015.

Allan R. Millett, Peter Maslowski, and William B. Feis — *For the Common Defense: A Military History of the United States from 1607 to 2012*. 3rd Ed. New York: Free Press, 2012.

Mark I. Nickerson and Joshua S. Goldstein — *The Wounds Within: A Veteran, a PTSD Therapist, and a Nation Unprepared*. New York: Skyhorse Publishing, 2015.

Derek S. Reveron and Judith Hicks Stiehm — *Inside Defense: Understanding the US Military in the 21st Century*. New York: Palgrave Macmillan, 2013.

Howard Schultz and Rajiv Chandrasekaran
For Love of Country: What Our Veterans Can Teach Us About Citizenship, Heroism, and Sacrifice. New York: Alfred A. Knopf, 2014.

Bashir Shah
Muslim and in the US Military. Bloomington, IN: AuthorHouse, 2010.

Nancy Sherman
Afterwar: Healing the Moral Wounds of Our Soldiers. New York: Oxford University Press, 2015.

Stephen Snyder-Hill
Soldier of Change: From the Closet to the Forefront of the Gay Rights Movement. Lincoln: University of Nebraska Press, 2014.

Judith Hicks Stiehm
The US Military: A Basic Introduction. New York: Routledge, 2012.

Jennifer Morrison Taw
Mission Revolution: The U.S. Military and Stability Operations. New York: Columbia University Press, 2015.

Index

N

S